CARTWHEELS

IN THE

Rain

CARTWHEELS

IN THE

Rain

Finding Faith in the Wake
of the Unthinkable

Joseph Dubowski

DPI
DISCIPLESHIP
PUBLICATIONS
INTERNATIONAL

www.dpibooks.org

Cartwheels in the Rain
©2010 by DPI Books
5016 Spedale Court #331
Spring Hill, TN 37174

Printed in the United States of America

Cover Design: Brian Branch
Cover Image: ©iStockphotos/BobIngelhart
Interior Design: Thais Gloor

ISBN: 978-1-57782-258-5

First of all, I dedicate this book to Laurel Ann—
my wife,
my best friend,
and my partner through this journey.

I would also like to remember and pay tribute to the memories of Gayle's classmates, especially those who shared in her fate that cold February day. I, like so many, have the misfortune to learn about them only after that day, and with their families, wish to do what I can to ensure that these special people are never forgotten.

Catalina Garcia
Catalina was a sophomore majoring in elementary education at Northern Illinois University, and very active in the Latino Resource Center. She will always be remembered for her optimism, her zest for life and her fun-lovingness. Her brother, Jaime, remembers that "[She] was our princess in pink. She loved pink. She loved everything in life."

Daniel Parmenter
Daniel, who stood about 6' 4", was described as a "gentle giant," a young man who loved sports, and enjoyed playing rugby and football. Known for his good humor and strong work ethic, Daniel was majoring in finance and working as an advertising representative for The Northern Star (the student newspaper at NIU) the semester when the shooting took place. He was also a member of the Pi Kappa Alpha fraternity, and made many friends there. His smile, his

warmth, his intelligence and common sense, and his eagerness to learn are deeply missed. His memory will inspire many to follow as his life touched everyone who knew him.

Julianna Gehant

Julianna was a lover of children and a member of a close-knit family in Mendota, Illinois. Before attending NIU as an elementary education major, she served her country for twelve years in the U.S. Army and Army Reserves. Her service included a tour of duty in Bosnia, and she attained the rank of Sergeant First Class. After gaining some experience teaching during her military service, she found a career path for herself to follow, and chose NIU for her education. She was kind, fun-loving and conscientious—the type of person who made life more fun for those around her. She enjoyed country music and was beginning to take an interest in ballroom dancing—always learning new things.

Ryanne Mace

Ryanne was an intelligent, funny and compassionate young woman who could be counted upon by friends for her sound and level-headed advice. It was her concern for the disenfranchised person and those in need that led her to major in psychology, with the intent of one day obtaining a doctorate-level degree and focusing professionally on counseling. She loved to learn, to study French and play violin in her high school orchestra, and loved to read. At the same time, she was a typical college student who liked to stay up late and sleep in, and was not above waiting in line to be among the first to buy the next Harry Potter book.

Contents

Introduction

The small group of college students gathered in the dining area on the ground floor of the Holmes Student Center at Northern Illinois University, getting ready for a Bible study. Most of the students felt gloomy because it was beginning to rain, and some of them groaned at the prospect of getting wet. But Gayle Dubowski, a sophomore, was excited.

"I like to do cartwheels in the rain," she told Anthony Testa. Anthony, looking outside at the downpour, turned to her and said, "Okay, Gayle. There's no way you're going to do a cartwheel right now." But before the words were out of his mouth, Gayle was bolting for the door—and while the others stood and looked on, warm and dry inside, she did a cartwheel in the rain.

It is April 11, 2008—nearly two months after the shooting at Northern Illinois University in which Gayle was killed, and it happens to be my birthday. I sit at our dining room table with my journal in front of me, alone. I stare out the window at the rain blowing against the windowpane. I think of Gayle.

I feel like she is beckoning me to come join her outside, to enjoy the spring rain, to feel its cold freshness, to relish life for its own sake, to get soaked to the bone in my pajamas.

I continue to sit and stare, my stubborn practical self—yet I feel something stirring in my heart.

The rain continues, only harder. She is calling to me to come outside and join her, but I can't. I tell her so out loud as tears roll down my cheeks and I stay fixed to my chair. I can't go out and join her—not yet. I'm not ready. The rain subsides for a moment, as if it is sad. Then it starts again, as if Gayle were saying, "Are you sure?" I nod my head, and moments later the rain stops.

My wife returns with the groceries. I dry my face and help her put them away.

On Thursday, February 14, 2008, a shooting took place on the campus of Northern Illinois University—a multiple murder that forever changed the lives of many families, especially the families of those who perished. Since that shooting, there have been other incidents of violence in which people of all ages have died, and the end of pain and tragedy in the world is not in sight.

This book is about more than surviving and living with loss. It is about more than the impact of one brief, humble life on a family and the world. It is especially about finding and holding on to faith in the wake of the unthinkable. It is about working through the pain of loss and disappointment and finding that after the work is done, you might be inspired to do cartwheels in the rain—even if you have never done cartwheels before and even if the storm had threatened to wash you away.

Part 1

The Storm

Security is mostly a superstition; it does not exist in nature, nor do the children of men as a whole experience it. Avoiding danger is no safer in the long run than outright exposure. Life is either a daring adventure or nothing.

—Marcel Proust

1

Gayle, Interrupted

"I love you! I missed you. I want to spend time with you," *said Gayle to Robin Weidner as she entered the room and ran* *up to greet her at the Weidners' home the night of February* *13, 2008. Robin and her husband, David, were hosting a* *group of college students and young adults in DeKalb,* *Illinois, near the NIU campus. Robin had just returned from* *a business trip, and Gayle told her that night that she want-* *ed to get to know her better.*

Gayle was in her second year of school at NIU, and while *she was not necessarily homesick, she told Robin that she felt* *perhaps she could use a "second mother" in DeKalb, someone* *she could confide in and learn from. They talked about a* *time when they could get together, and eventually decided* *upon Friday afternoon, the day after Valentine's Day.*

During the devotional that followed, she took notes from *the Bible lesson on "God's Attributes." Among the Scriptures* *she noted in her journal was Luke 4:16, to which she com-* *mented, "He came to set everyone free." For Romans 8:1,* *which states "Therefore, now there is no condemnation for* *those who are in Christ Jesus," she wrote, "God created me to* *be free like a bird!* *"*

✢

On Valentine's Day morning Gayle awakened late after

staying up studying for a test. She trudged sleepily up the stairs from her bedroom in the basement and into the kitchen of the townhouse she shared with four friends. A couple of her roommates who were in the living room heard her walk past the doorway and go to the refrigerator, and called out to her "Happy Valentine's Day, Gayle!" She responded to their cheerful greeting with some mumbling about it not being a "real holiday," but only one made up to sell greeting cards.

One of the girls asked her if she got up on the wrong side of the bed. This was met by a moment of silence. Then, suddenly, Gayle reappeared in the doorway to the living room with a big smile on her face and cried out "Happy Valentine's Day, Girls!"

Her roommates asked, "Starting over again are we, Gayle?"

Thus Gayle began the morning—a story that would not surprise her parents when they heard about it the next day. What would surprise them was the grocery bags full of refreshments they found beside her bed. In spite of Gayle's mixed feelings about Valentine's Day, she was planning and organizing a surprise event for Friday night, in which the single women would encourage the single men with food and games. She was very excited about doing something special for her "brothers" in the church, and had a lot of fun shopping for the event.

After returning to her room and getting dressed, Gayle sat down on her bed and opened her Bible to read and to pray for her day. In her journal she wrote, simply:

→ Valentine's Day Psalm 141:3
"Set a guard over my heart, O Lord; keep watch over
the door of my lips. Let not my heart be drawn to
what is evil."

Often she would take time to write her prayers in her
journal, but on Thursdays this semester she had a 9:30 AM
class (Intermediate Russian) followed by an hour-and-a-
half break for lunch and study, followed by two back-to-
back classes in the afternoon. So, after jotting down this
scripture, she prayed as she packed her backpack and the
red cloth shoulder-bag she used as a purse (she never liked
to carry a real purse) and made her way up the stairs to
leave for class.

On her way out of the house, one of her roommates
stopped her and remarked how pretty and unusually blue
her eyes looked that morning. "Did you put on some different eyeliner this morning, Gayle?"

"No," she responded, thanked her, and wished her
roommates a great day. Then she left her roommates and
townhouse for what would be the last time.

*Gayle's high school
senior picture*

2

The Clouds Gather

Roughly forty miles east of DeKalb, at our home in Carol Stream, Illinois, Gayle's mother, Laurel, and brother, Ryan, and I were enjoying a peaceful Valentine's Day, never imagining what we would face by the time the day was finished. I drove Ryan to school that morning. Having been laid off from my job three weeks earlier, I returned home to resume my job search, enjoy some time with Laurel, and celebrate the day together.

I spent most of the day exchanging emails with a recruiter and making adjustments to my résumé. After stopping to enjoy lunch together, Laurel and I sat down on the couch and exchanged Valentine's gifts. I gave her a perfumed lotion and cologne set, and she gave me a CD set by the recording artist Mark Schultz. She told me that she thought I would enjoy a song on the CD called "Walking Her Home," and she asked me to play it.

The song was about a young man who takes a girl out on her very first date and falls in love with her that night as he was walking her home. It was a very romantic song, and we enjoyed listening to it together.

As we sat on the couch holding each other close and listening to the music, my mind wandered to thoughts about our own romance. I thought back through the twenty-five years we had been together, through all the memories we shared. I remembered our first date, the day I proposed to her, and the births of our two children. I saw us raising them together, and imagined life after they were gone, when once more it would be just the two of us. I dreamed of playing together with our grandchildren someday. And I imagined growing old, patiently enduring each other's aches and pains, and going into eternity—walking home together.

After the song was over, we kissed and talked for a while, sharing our thoughts and dreams with each other. Then we got back to work: I with my job search, she with her household chores.

Laurel left at around 3 PM to pick Ryan up from school. I noticed that a couple of friends had sent me job leads, and so I stayed in my basement office and answered their emails. I sent off a couple more replies, and then prepared to log off my computer for the day. But before I did, I noticed the subject line of a new email message from the *Chicago Tribune*: "Tribune Alerts: Shooting Reported at NIU."

I immediately opened the message and clicked on the link to the *Tribune's* website. The story was very fresh, and there was little information—not even a photograph—so I knew it must have just occurred. I wanted to know more.

My initial thought was along the lines of, "I wonder if Gayle knows about this." I thought of her and the dozen or so students in her campus group with the DeKalb Church of Christ, and hoped that none of them were involved. I decided to run upstairs to turn on the radio and learn more about what had happened. As I began climbing the stairs, the memory of the story of the terrible shooting at Virginia Tech from just ten months earlier came to mind. I uttered a quick prayer that nothing that terrible had happened again.

I turned on the radio in our family room to see if they were reporting the event yet. As I tuned in the station, I heard a young woman—a student from the class where the shooting took place—talking to the host. The caller said that a young man carrying a guitar case entered the lecture hall by way of the stage door just about five or ten minutes before the class was supposed to end. He pulled a shotgun out of the case and began firing it into the class; everyone started yelling and screaming, running to escape from the classroom. She told about running straight to her off-campus apartment and calling the news station to get the word out to as many people as possible.

Listening to her story, I tried to get a feeling for how many casualties there might have been, and tried to learn whether the person doing the shooting was working alone or with someone else. I also wanted to know where the shooting took place. I didn't remember Gayle's class schedule, though, and the name of the building did not sound familiar.

It was around this time that Laurel returned with Ryan. I quickly briefed them on the news and turned on the TV. Laurel and Ryan suggested calling Gayle to see if she was okay, so I tried to reach her on her cell phone. She did not pick up the call, so I left a brief message asking her to return my call as soon as she got my message. In case she was in a class or somewhere she could not talk, I asked Ryan to text her, which he did. Though no reply came to us from Gayle, we reasoned that she might have left her phone charging in her bedroom, or might have forgotten to turn it on that morning, rather than think there could be a possible connection between her and the news we were hearing.

As we made these calls to Gayle, the helicopter from the TV station arrived on the scene, training its camera on the visitors' parking lot in the heart of the campus where police cars, fire equipment and ambulances were stationed outside Cole Hall.

Not remembering Gayle's class schedule for the spring term, I tried to remember what kind of classes Cole Hall held. While I tried to find where I had written down Gayle's schedule, Laurel began preparing to leave for the studio where she taught piano on Thursday nights, as she had done for some seventeen years. As she did, friends and relatives watching or listening to the news began to call us to find out if we had heard about the shooting, and to find out if Gayle was okay. All three of us began answering calls and reassuring people that it was unlikely, with a campus that size, that Gayle was involved in any way, and promised to let everyone know Gayle was okay when we heard from her.

Meanwhile, I remembered the map of the NIU campus we received during freshman orientation. I found the map in a folder we kept in our pantry and located Cole Hall— right in the middle of the campus, less than two blocks from Gayle's townhouse. I felt a pang of concern as I thought that Gayle might have passed by the hall on the way home from class, or even heard shots fired as far away as her apartment. Still, I had no idea what classes Gayle had that afternoon, nor did I know if any of her classes were taught there. So, I quickly chased away my anxiety in favor of the odds against our daughter's being in any immediate danger. I said good-bye to Laurel and told her I would let her know the minute I heard anything from Gayle.

About a half hour after Laurel left for work, Chris Zillman—the minister for the church in DeKalb that Gayle belonged to—called us. "Have you heard from Gayle?" he asked.

"No, Chris. Not yet," I replied, trying to sound nonchalant. "We left a voice message for her, and Ryan texted her, but no word yet. Have you heard from her? Is everyone accounted for out there?"

"So far we have heard from everyone but Gayle and one other girl. Do you know whether she had classes this afternoon, and where they were?" Chris asked.

"No. I was just looking for her class schedule, and haven't found it yet," I said. "Sometimes she turns her phone off and forgets about it, or leaves it back in the apartment. So I'm not really worried that she hasn't returned my call."

Chris said, "I'm going over to the girls' apartment to see if she's there and just not picking up her phone. I'll call you back in a few minutes," and hung up. (Gayle and her four roommates were members of the same church.)

Learning the location of the building where the shooting took place followed closely by receiving Chris's call did not reassure me that Gayle was all right. Pacing back and forth in the dining and family rooms—listening to the TV echoing the story with the paucity of information the reporters had over and over again—made me anxious to hear from her.

Finally I remembered writing down in my planner the times and classes that Gayle had sent me. Finding it, I read Gayle's class schedule:

Gayle's S2: MWF   1300-1350   World Regnl Geog
MW   1600-1715   Classical Myth.
T Th   0930-1045   Intermediate Russian
1230-1345   Intro Cultur. Anthro.
1400-1515   Intro Ocean Science

Decoding my shorthand and abbreviations, I found that Gayle had a class that matched—time-wise—the description I had heard on the radio. *Intro to Ocean Science* ended at 3:15, the time the class where the shooting occurred was supposed to have ended. Then I remembered one of the people interviewed on the radio saying that the class where the shooting occurred was an oceanography class.

As I digested this information, Chris called a second time from DeKalb. This time, he sounded more concerned and apologetic. "Joe, I'm at Gayle's townhouse now, and I've spoken to her roommates. We found a copy of her schedule in her room. Joe—I'm sorry, but I think that Gayle was in that class."

There was silence on my end of the line for a moment. "Okay. Thanks," I said. "But that doesn't necessarily mean she was hurt, though. Perhaps she ran out of the classroom with everyone else and left her phone. She could be hiding somewhere, or she could be talking to the police as a witness."

"No one here has heard from Gayle yet," Chris replied.

"I'm going over to Cole Hall and see if I can talk to the police there, and see if I can learn anything from them. I'll call you as soon as I learn anything."

"Thanks, Chris," I responded. "If I hear anything more before then, I'll be sure to call you."

"You might want to call Kishwaukee Community Hospital," Chris suggested. "They'll be taking the wounded there."

"Thanks, Chris," I said. "I'll do that."

I told Ryan what Chris had told me. He was answering text messages from friends on his phone, one right after another. In addition, our home line was ringing every few minutes. I tried to answer as many of the calls as I could, but my mind and attention were being drawn elsewhere.

Following Chris's advice, I found the hospital's website and a page that gave information on the shooting and the number of victims brought in to them so far. No names were listed; nor did I expect them to be. By the time I found the page, they said that seventeen people had been transported to the hospital for treatment. No one admitted to the hospital had died yet, but one of the victims had been airlifted to a trauma center in nearby Rockford. They provided a number for people to call and find out more details.

Calling the number given on the website, I left a message and my contact information. The hospital promised to contact people when information and personnel were available. Meanwhile, Chris spoke with police on the scene and found that they had no word on Gayle or her whereabouts. He then called and told me he would keep trying to find her, and would let me know when she turned up.

The Weidners called around this time and offered to go to the hospital on our behalf to see if Gayle had been taken there. Robin later called back to tell us that the hospital did not have any record of admitting Gayle or anyone matching her description. She offered to wait at the hospital until we could get to DeKalb ourselves, and I thanked her.

While we waited, hoping that Gayle was hiding somewhere, or for some reason had skipped class that afternoon to read in the library, all our friends felt the need to call us and hear us say that Gayle was okay and that there was no need to worry. It was encouraging to know so many people cared and that so many were looking out for us in case we had missed the news. Still, I felt anxiety growing with each passing minute. The thing I was most afraid of at the time was that she had run out of the classroom and was hiding somewhere, perhaps in shock and too afraid to come out of hiding. The thought of Gayle being afraid—or of anything scaring her—unsettled me. This made me want to go out to DeKalb immediately to be there for her, but I didn't want to go without Laurel.

Around 6:30 I called my dad and asked him if he'd heard the news. I told him that I did not know anything of Gayle's whereabouts, but would call him when I knew she was all right.

By approximately 7:30, I heard from Kishwaukee Community Hospital. They told me that no one named Gayle had been identified among the wounded at their facility. They wished me the best, and told me they would keep my number handy should any information become available about her.

Laurel and I talked over the phone, and I told her that Ryan and I would be ready to leave as soon as she returned. She was trying to remain calm and get through the night, but the waiting and not knowing were tearing her apart.

At last, just before 8:00 PM, Laurel got home from work. She immediately set about putting together a care package for Gayle, to encourage her when she turned up at the townhouse. We also prepared ourselves for the possibility that Gayle was frightened—or worse, turned up among the wounded. We agreed we would plan on spending the night with her in DeKalb or be ready to bring her home. However, we stopped short of actually packing overnight bags and toothbrushes. Laurel just packed a bag full of fresh fruit, bottled water and diet tea drinks, and then we were ready to go.

Jeff Balsom, one of the leaders of our church and a close friend, called while Laurel was getting ready. He had been talking to Chris Zillman and asked if there was anything we needed. I just told him to pray for Gayle and for all the other families and victims. I told him we were leaving for DeKalb to look for and be with her. He asked if we'd like him to accompany us. I thanked him for the offer, but did not think it would be necessary. I told him he was welcome to meet us there if he wanted to, though, and he told me that he would—because that's what friends are for.

After hanging up, I imagined us all arriving in DeKalb and overwhelming Gayle with love, and I thought about how encouraged (and maybe embarrassed) she would feel from seeing so many people show up on her doorstep on a moment's notice—assuming she came home uninjured. Any other outcome was unthinkable.

We left for DeKalb soon after Jeff's call. It was such a relief just getting on the road after waiting and watching the news for four hours. I wanted so badly to get out to DeKalb to look for Gayle myself, to see the scene where the shooting had taken place—to feel like I could *do* something and not simply wait for and rely on others.

3

The Storm Builds

I had always looked forward to going to DeKalb to see Gayle and visit with other friends in the church. But as we drove that night, I felt myself gripping the wheel more and more tightly with the anxiety growing as I recapped what we knew so far. I did so mostly for Laurel's sake, as she had been working all evening: seventeen wounded taken to area hospitals, five dead, including the gunman, and one air-lifted to Rockford. As we talked about the numbers, the math began to bother me more when Ryan mentioned that he had last heard that *six* had died. I pressed down harder on the gas pedal and drove on in silence, hope giving way to dread inside me as we approached DeKalb.

When we arrived at Gayle's townhouse around 9:20 PM, we found the living room filled with her roommates and her friends, all looking grim and worried. I was hoping to find Chris Zillman there, but was told he was at home. When I got no answer at his home number, I tried to reach him on his cell phone.

"Hi, Chris," I said when he answered. "We just got to Gayle's place. Any news for us?"

"The police told us they're trying to identify some of the victims," Chris replied, "and are telling families who don't know the whereabouts of their kids to go to the hospital for questioning. Do you know where Kishwaukee Hospital is?"

"I have no idea. But I'm sure someone here can give us directions."

"Good," said Chris. "I'll meet you over there in a few minutes."

"Bye, Chris. And thanks," I replied as I hung up and started asking for directions. I asked Gayle's roommates if someone would ride with us to make sure we didn't get lost. Two of them quickly volunteered, and we gave the care package we'd brought for Gayle to the others and left for the hospital.

About ten minutes later, we arrived at the hospital. The Weidners embraced us as we entered the door. They had been waiting there for nearly four hours. Moments later, Chris arrived, accompanied by Jeff Balsom and two other ministers from our church. A police sergeant from the NIU campus police, Jeanne Meyers, introduced herself, along with another officer from the DeKalb Police Department. They explained that they were interviewing parents to try to identify the victims of the shooting. It turns out that many—if not most—of the victims (especially the female victims) had been transported without any identification, and they asked if they could meet with us privately to ask us some questions about Gayle.

We were ushered into the hallway of an office portion of the hospital, where they offered us chairs and water. The DeKalb County Coroner came and explained the situation to us.

There were five students plus the gunman who had been killed. Three of the victims were women who had been pronounced dead at the scene immediately following the shooting. The FBI had taken over the investigation of the shooting, and wouldn't allow anyone other than law enforcement officials to enter Cole Hall to identify the victims. They needed us to give them some way of identifying Gayle (clothing, jewelry, birthmarks, tattoos, etc.) to see if she was among the dead at the scene.

Holding on to what little optimism we had left, we described Gayle's physical attributes: about 5 feet 1 inch; 135 pounds; dark brown hair, just short of shoulder length; blue eyes. We asked Gayle's roommates to tell them what she was wearing that day. They told the coroner about the wristwatch she usually wore and the silver necklace on which she wore her birthstone ring, along with a dove charm with "Peace" engraved in it, and one other charm.

Equipped with this information, the coroner and police officers left us to find out if any of the victims at the scene matched that description. Meanwhile, Ms. Meyers escorted us to a more comfortable place to wait for news. While everyone else went into the conference room, I stopped in the hallway and called my sister, Liz, in New York City. We cried and talked for a few minutes, and I promised to call and let her know what we learned from the authorities. I also called friends in the small group we led in the church back home, and asked them to spread the word and ask for prayers for us.

Laurel's eyes met mine as I entered the conference room, both of us silently expressing our hope that we would be reunited with Gayle any moment and that this nightmare would end. But as minutes passed, the anxiety in the room mounted. The room began to fill with more friends as others joined in our vigil, wanting to be with and support us—and hoping to hear good news as well.

At around 10:25 PM, NIU President, John Peters, and his Vice President of Operations came to see us to express their deepest sorrow at the events of the day and offer their support. I recognized both men from the press conference on television earlier in the day. I thanked them for their sympathy, but expressed the lingering hope we wouldn't be needing it.

But a few minutes after they left—some seven-and-a-half hours after the first shot had been fired in Cole Hall—the coroner returned with one of the officers from the university. "We checked the description you gave us against those of the three girls at Cole Hall, and the description doesn't match any of the women in the classroom," he told us. As I tried to digest that news, he continued. "However, one of the victims brought here was airlifted to St. Anthony's Trauma Center in Rockford. The doctors there worked for about forty-five minutes, but were unable to save her. We talked to the people up there in Rockford, and the girl matches the description you gave…"

The room erupted in tears and cries of grief and pain. Laurel, Ryan and I grabbed and held onto each other as the wave of agony washed over us, overwhelming us. We were surrounded and hugged by friends who cried with us. Everyone hugged and held whoever they could, trying to find strength in one another. The waiting was over—but our ordeal had just begun.

Once again able to speak, we questioned the coroner further, looking for some ray of hope, some chance of a mistake. But as we questioned him, it seemed more and more likely that Gayle was dead. The coroner asked if we would like to identify her ourselves, and we both insisted that we see the body before we would be convinced.

Suddenly the clocks seemed to speed up. The waiting that made minutes seem like hours gave way to people asking questions and making decisions about what to do and about who was going where and with whom. I was confronted with a drive to a coroner's office in an unfamiliar city in the middle of the night; figuring out who we wanted to go with and who would drive; and calling people to let them know Gayle was probably among the dead.

At the same time, others in the room were making plans to get the entire church in DeKalb together at the Zillmans' house to break the news and pray together. Other people asked if they could follow us to Rockford. Laurel's sister, Kathleen, and her husband, Jim, planned to meet us there as well. Their support through those first few weeks would prove most helpful and encouraging.

I felt like I was in a dream. None of this seemed real. I felt like I was watching all this unfold from the outside, unable to withstand the shock that Gayle was dead, that all of this was really happening, or had really happened. A certain detachment came over me as I told myself that mistakes were still possible. I remembered the story of two college girls, who looked very much alike, being involved in a terrible car crash with one dying and the other being comatose; their identities were mistaken until the surviving one, still swollen from the accident, was able to write her name. At that moment, I was still hoping there was a mistake, and that the unfortunate girl in Rockford was someone else's daughter.

Laurel and I got directions and left for Rockford as the DeKalb County Coroner arranged for someone to receive us in about an hour. We asked the Weidners to ride with us, and Jeff, along with the ministers from our local church, told us they would meet us there.

We were comforted to have the Weidners drive with us as we were not alone with our own torturous thoughts. The drive itself helped to calm me and distract me as well. We finally arrived in Rockford after midnight. Upon finding the building, we were glad to see that Jeff and the ministers from our local church had arrived before us and were able to show us where to park. A guard was waiting to admit us. The Winnebago County Coroner and a couple of her assistants were expecting us, and they escorted us down the stairs to the basement.

Along the way to Rockford, I considered whether or not I wanted to see the body. I did not want my memory of Gayle, if the body was Gayle's, to be scarred by visions of disfigurement. So, as we followed the coroner to the basement, I asked her what to expect. As we entered a small, undecorated room with a couple of folding tables and a few chairs in the middle, she assured us that the girl's face was not disfigured and that the wounds were all covered. She warned us that the girl's eyelids looked bruised due to the blood that had collected in the capillaries behind the eyelids. She also explained that we would only be able to see her face and neck; everything else was covered. With that, she and an assistant, a chaplain, led us into a room off to our left and turned on the lights.

On the table just inside to the left of the doorway was a small woman's body covered in white sheets and a thin blanket, exposing only her face and neck for us to see. Around her neck was a silver chain, and on the chain were a birthstone ring and the other charms that we told the coroner in DeKalb to look for. Her hair was pulled back from her face and hidden under the sheet they had wrapped snuggly around her head. Her skin was pale and lifeless, and her eyelids gave the appearance of a pair of "black eyes." Her face had a look of peace about it, with her mouth betraying neither a smile nor a frown—more a tired peace of sleep. Laurel and I burst into tears as we realized the girl on the table was Gayle.

I had to look away, and I stepped aside so that Laurel and Ryan could get a better look at her. I buried my face in the sheets around her legs and began to cry like I had never cried before. One of my friends placed his hand on my shoulder, trying to control his own emotions, and said in the most consoling way he could, "Your job is done." I continued to cry uncontrollably, gasping for breath, barely making out what he said as he explained: "You've done what all of us long to do. She made it, and she's with God now."

I could not take those words in. Racing through my mind came memories of the life of the baby we named Gayle Marie. All I could see was twenty years of a relationship come to a terrible end, along with an end to all my hopes, dreams and expectations for our future together.

4

More Than an Ordinary Girl

Gayle Marie Dubowski was born on Tuesday, September 29, 1987, at approximately 9:26 PM—our first child. She was born with a thin shock of dark brown hair on her little round head, which over the course of several weeks gave way to a full head of blonde hair.

My fears as a new father were of changing diapers, cleaning spit-up, and incessant crying (the baby's). Somehow we were blessed with a baby girl who seldom spit up and only cried when she was hungry or frustrated with something. The diaper thing—well, my love for her overcame that, and I lent a hand in changing whenever needed.

During the first couple weeks of her life, she slept in a bassinette at the foot of our bed. That did not last very long, however—not because she would cry in the middle of the night, but because even the slightest sound she made would awaken me. Sound sleeper that I was before she was born, I became a very light sleeper after her birth and remained that way for several months. Soon she was sleeping in her own bedroom so that her mother and I could get *some* rest.

"Joe, could you please check on Gayle?" Laurel cried from the kitchen. Gayle (who was perhaps six months old at the time) had been fussing in her room, and Laurel was trying to make dinner. As I like to eat and didn't feel like

Baby Gayle Marie

trading places with her in the kitchen, I obediently went to Gayle's room to try and cheer her up.

I picked Gayle up and put her in a little swinging chair in her bedroom. She continued to complain, and so I looked around her room for something to entertain her with. I found a small inflated beach ball, and pretended to juggle it up in the air, purposely missing it and letting it fall on my head. I would then fall down on the floor and watch the ball roll away from me. She stopped crying and fussing and started to watch my silliness with the ball. After I repeated this a couple of times, she started to giggle; after a few more misses, and seeing me act more and more frustrated with this uncooperative ball, she began laughing almost hysterically. For the next twenty years, I lived to make Gayle laugh.

Looking out the window of our apartment months later at the first snow of the season, I thought it would be fun to introduce Gayle to snow. She had begun to walk only a couple months earlier, and had no memory of the white stuff from her first winter.

Calling her to the window, I pointed at the white-blanketed outdoors and asked her what she thought of it. "Would you like to go outside with me?" I asked. She merely looked out the window and put her thumb in her mouth.

"Come on. Let's get dressed, and I'll show you snow," I said.

Grabbing her tiny pink coat and scarf, and a pair of tiny shoes she had for playing outside, I bundled her the best I could and then got myself dressed for the adventure. She didn't like getting dressed in a heavy winter coat, but tolerated it for this occasion. Once dressed, I told Laurel we would be back in a few minutes, and picked Gayle up and headed out the door.

Setting foot outside on the mild winter day, I held Gayle in one arm and held out the other so she could see the snow land in my palm and melt. She watched. I gently removed her thumb-hand from her mouth (we tried to discourage thumb-sucking, but to no avail) and held it out to catch the soft flakes. She felt the flakes drop into her palm and melt, but made no comment. She just returned the thumb where it belonged.

Gayle bundled up to go out into the snow

I decided to set her down to let her explore on her own. But as I bent down, she quickly withdrew her thumb from her mouth and threw her arms around my neck. Her eyes had grown very big, and she tried to bury her face in my scarf. She was afraid of stepping in the snow!

"Gayle, what's the matter?" I asked. "Don't you want to walk in the snow?" She just stared out at the flakes. So, to test the theory, I stepped back under the cover of the entrance to the building and tried again to set her down, and she stood there with no protest.

"Gayle, it's okay. It's just snow. See? It turns into water in my hand. Tell you what, why don't you take my hand and we can walk together," I said. Then taking her tiny hand, I took a step forward onto the sidewalk; she stayed put, feet planted firmly on the porch.

Eventually—not that day, but eventually—Gayle grew to love going out in the snow. I don't remember how she changed her mind about it, but she did. Funny thing is, this scene was repeated four months later with our first trip to a playground with sand in it.

"There's Gayle Marie. Gayle, say hi to the camera," I said as I tried to video our family's Labor Day party on Lake Mary in Wisconsin. She just paused by the refreshment cart on the patio, looked at me, and giggled. The family was celebrating Gayle's birthday (her fourth) as well as her cousin Tory's.

Asking her to tell us how old she was, she merely held up four fingers and grinned. She was the quietest person at the party that day.

Getting ready for company one evening in the townhouse we had moved to, I helped Laurel by setting the table. For some reason, I decided to move Gayle's high chair to the end of the table opposite where she usually sat, so it was facing the kitchen and the black china cabinet. When it was time to eat, I lifted Gayle up and tried to seat her in her chair. All of a sudden, she threw both arms around my neck and refused to let me put her in the chair.

"Gayle," I said, surprised. "What's the matter, Honey?"

She looked back at me with fear in her eyes and pointed to the opposite end of the dining room. "Daddy, the frogs!" she cried.

Looking toward the other end of the room, I tried to see what she was so afraid of. I didn't see anything resembling a frog. I asked her, "The *frogs*?" I thought that I misunderstood her, but she nodded and repeated, "The frogs," and held on to me even tighter and looked away.

Laurel came into the room to see what was going on, and the two of us began looking for the frogs. We asked her to point them out to us, but she refused to go near the place where she was pointing—our china cabinet. We were on the verge of giving up trying to figure out what she was scared of when it dawned on me what she saw—the handles on the drawers to the cabinet. The brass handles were in the shape of a smile, and each "smile" ended on either side with enlarged round knobs that attached to the drawers, resem-

Gayle at three years old

bling "eyes"—the handles themselves were the golden, smiling frogs that were staring at Gayle and scaring her.

I went over to the cabinet and pointed at one of the handles and asked her, "Are these the frogs you are talking about?" She looked at me with her big blue eyes and nodded. Laurel and I couldn't help but laugh—

and hugged her to let her know the frogs were friendly and were harmless.

Ariel the mermaid is getting married to Eric the prince as four-year-old Gayle and I watch the video of *The Little Mermaid* for the hundredth time since someone gave it to her. Sitting there watching the movie with her I imagined, as King Poseidon entered the scene, giving Gayle away to someone someday.

Then, out of the blue, her eyes still fixed on the screen, Gayle says, "Will you marry me, Daddy?"

Suddenly, I am the prince, and I feel like a king.

These and a hundred other memories flooded my mind as I poured my tears out into the sheets covering Gayle's now lifeless form. My friend's statement that my "work is finished" with Gayle brought back the memories of lying on the floor of her bedroom late into the nights nearly four years earlier, while she lay in bed asking me questions concerning what I believed about God and becoming a follower of Jesus. I remembered baptizing her days later; some of the people in the room with me that night had witnessed her baptism as well.

Realizing now that I would never get to walk her down the aisle and into the arms of a special someone; that I would never hold her babies in my arms; that I wouldn't have her to comfort me as I got old, as I was doing for my father—all these thoughts were more than I could bear. I didn't *want* my job to be finished! Instead I protested in my heart, "It isn't supposed to end this way! Lord, why did you let this happen?"

As I collected my thoughts during the hours that followed, I remembered back to the night before, and wondered if the plans that I had the previous afternoon were changed by God in order to prepare me for this night. I had planned to go to a meeting in order to make some new contacts to help me in my search for work. Instead, I was delayed by my father's doctor appointments and ended up attending our Bible study group, where we watched an episode from a DVD series entitled *Does God Exist* as part of our study. The program was entitled "The Problem of Human Suffering" and dealt with the question of whether the presence of suffering in the world is compatible with faith in the existence of a loving and merciful God.

The creator of the series, a science teacher and former atheist, was able to share about how he and his wife struggled with questions about God's existence and love while wrestling with why their child was born with autism, when they believed in a loving and caring Creator. Didn't the unfairness of their suffering point to flaws in their faith?

Remembering what I heard that night *did* help me this night. As I stood in the room looking at Gayle's still body, I thought about trusting and believing in God. I thought of asking God, "Why? WHY? This isn't the way it is supposed to end." But, at the same time, I felt like I could hear God asking *me* the question: "Do you trust me? Do you *still* trust me?"

I knew I had just lost someone who meant so very much to me. Losing my trust in God meant still a greater loss. I felt that if I lost that, too, I would have no one to turn to—no one who could truly understand what I was feeling the way he could, no one who could give me reason to live another day.

Even though we didn't reach Rockford until close to midnight, others came to see Gayle and be with us even later. Kathleen and Jim joined us first, and then one of our friends brought his daughter, Allison, to be there for Ryan (they had grown up together and were good friends). We stayed and spent time trying to make the most of some of the last minutes we would ever have with Gayle's body, trying to comprehend the tragedy.

At last we gathered together and prayed, and then people began to depart and go home. The Weidners offered to let us spend the night at their home in DeKalb rather than make the long drive back home, and we gratefully accepted. We were exhausted and would have found it difficult to concentrate on driving home after what we had just been through.

Meanwhile, back home in Carol Stream and in the Zillmans' home in DeKalb, many of Gayle's and our closest friends gathered to comfort and console one another. They spent time trying to come to grips with their loss, told stories they remembered about Gayle and prayed for us.

Just before 4 AM, the three of us were as settled as we could be—Ryan on the couch downstairs and Laurel and me in their daughter's bed. We both cried ourselves to a troubled sleep.

A new chapter in our lives was beginning.

5

The Waves Break

Waking up later in the morning after identifying Gayle's body, after only about four hours of sleep—eyes moist with fresh tears—we ate a breakfast provided by a friend who delivered it to the Weidners' house. We made plans to visit Gayle's room at the townhouse and collect some of the belongings we might need for the wake and the funeral. We would then make our way back toward the city to break the news to my father.

While visiting the townhouse, we talked with some of Gayle's roommates about her last morning at home. They shared with us about their last conversation with her, and about her planning a special night of encouragement for the young men in the church to be hosted by the single and college women—something that made me even more proud of her. We found the bags of paper goods and refreshments she had shopped for on the floor of her room by her bed. Her room was organized and clean, the way she left it the day before.

A Bible was lying open on her bed, and next to it was a black leather-bound journal. The Bible was open to the book of Psalms. Wondering what the last thing that she read was, Laurel and I opened her journal and read the entries from the previous two days, and held each other.

After catching her breath, Laurel began to gather

together some clothing for Gayle to wear for the visitation and funeral, along with her Bible, her journal and some jewelry. Meanwhile, Ryan and I found things that would remind us of Gayle and make us feel like a part of her was with us in the days to come. Then we said farewell to her roommates, thanked them for their help, and left to continue our homeward journey.

Before returning home, we wanted to break the news to my father. Along the way, a friend met us in order to bring Ryan back to our house, as a number of his friends were waiting there for him. After the difficult and painful work of telling my father the granddaughter he loved so much had been killed, we returned home to find a few dozen friends and neighbors waiting for us inside. Many had been there for hours, wanting to welcome us home and to care for our every need. We were overwhelmed by the display of love and support as all evening long more people came, bringing food, drinks, plants and flowers, and gifts. Friends came from more than two hours away to be with us, cry with us, to listen and to learn what had happened to Gayle.

Laurel and I were not prepared for such a reception. We hadn't eaten in probably eight hours; we had slept only four hours the night before; and we had just lived through the most difficult twenty-four hours of our lives. Now, arriving home to a houseful of guests, we did not know what to do. We found Ryan surrounded by a dozen or more friends in the basement.

We spent the next four hours greeting people as they came to see us, thanking people for coming as they left, and expending our remaining energy to make conversation and hold back the flood of pain and sorrow threatening to overwhelm us at any moment. Finally realizing how exhausted we were, I got everyone's attention and thanked them for coming and being there for us. I explained that we were exhausted, and that I needed to get Laurel upstairs and to bed before she collapsed. I told Ryan that a couple of his friends could spend the night with us. I then prayed with the group and asked people if they wouldn't mind letting themselves out while we went to bed.

Then, lying on our bed, Laurel and I cried ourselves to sleep once again.

The next six days left little time to process our grief. There were family members to notify, and there were arrangements to make and plans to carry out for the visitation, the private funeral and public memorial service. On top of the fact we were doing this for someone we thought would one day do it for us, we faced the facts that we had never done this before for anyone and were in no condition—emotionally, mentally or physically—to do it now.

What we really needed was to rest and talk through our feelings, but our feelings were too intense to handle. Waves of pain and sorrow would cascade and overwhelm us periodically, triggered by memories of things we had said to or done with Gayle, or things we had never taken the time to say or do. These waves left us feeling physically drained and emotionally fatigued. By noontime, we felt like we had worked a full day already.

Yet, in between the waves, we went about making plans,

arrangements and decisions with the help of friends and family: Whom would we invite to the funeral? Did we want a visitation on the day before the funeral or immediately before it? Did we want a public memorial service, and how many people did we think would attend? What kinds of flowers did we want? In the end, we decided on the personal things, and delegated many of the arrangements to others, reviewing and providing input as things progressed.

Saturday morning came, and as I remembered where I was, my eyes filled with tears once more. I dressed and went downstairs for breakfast.

Friends had locked up the house shortly after we went to bed the previous night. The main level of the house was neat and clean, although it was overflowing with trays of non-perishable foods (pastries, cookies, etc.), plates and napkins, plastic-ware, and the like, alongside the "projects in progress" piles I left on the dining room table two days earlier. People did a nice job cleaning and organizing the downstairs before leaving, and all the perishable food was crammed neatly into our refrigerator.

Before long the doorbell began ringing, and friends from far and near began arriving to see us and give to us. Somehow through it all, we managed to get out the door with Jeff and his wife, Roberta, to go to the funeral home to make final arrangements. Kathleen met us there.

At the funeral home, we had to address the practical aspects of ending our physical relationship with Gayle. We were given choices of flowers, caskets, burial versus cremation—and the list goes on. During those discussions, the full weight of what we were doing and talking about came to rest on me once more. The numbness that had protected me all day up until that point gave way to a fresh wave of grief—the thought of why we were there sinking in—and I had to excuse myself while the breakers overwhelmed me so others could continue the planning.

Finding an unoccupied room, I went in and sat down, grabbing a handful of tissues from the box on the desk. Jeff joined me and sat with me in silence while I shook my head and cried. I just could not stomach the fact that I was planning a funeral for my own daughter. At that time I thought about a passage quoted in Matthew 2:18:

> "A voice is heard in Ramah,
>   weeping and great mourning;
> Rachel weeping for her children
>   and refusing to be comforted,
> because they are no more."

This passage tells about the boys two years old and under being murdered at the command of King Herod, who was looking to destroy the child rumored to be the Messiah, thinking that he would be a future threat to his throne. I, too, felt like nothing would comfort me, nothing would remove the pain I felt now that Gayle was no longer there for me to call, to see, to touch.

Jeff listened to me tell him how I was feeling and explain how it hurt too much to think about what we were doing—for all this to happen so suddenly, so unexpectedly. Jeff asked if he could share with me something he had read in his own Bible study that morning. He read out of John 11, where Jesus was talking to Martha after Lazarus, her brother and his friend, had died:

"Lord," Martha said to Jesus, "if you had been here, my brother would not have died. But I know that even now God will give you whatever you ask."

Jesus said to her, "Your brother will rise again."

Martha answered, "I know he will rise again in the resurrection at the last day."

Jesus said to her, "I am the resurrection and the life. He who believes in me will live, even though he dies; and whoever lives and believes in me will never die. Do you believe this?"

"Yes, Lord," she told him, "I believe that you are the Christ, the Son of God, who was to come into the world." (John 11:21–27)

Jeff then spoke about what the passage meant to him: Gayle believed in Jesus, spoke up for him and lived for him, and therefore never really died. He found it comforting to know that Gayle was in paradise with Jesus. But when I did not feel comforted by that, it made me question my faith— did I *really believe* what Jesus said? Because I wasn't comforted at that moment, was my faith genuine? If it was, then why was I in such pain?

I used to ask that same question of Martha in the story: "Martha, don't you understand? Don't you believe? Your brother is in a better place." But suddenly I was in Martha's shoes, and facing Gayle's death from Martha's perspective: "Why didn't you save her, Jesus? If only she had not died (physically), we wouldn't be suffering."

Suddenly, I felt like I was standing there alongside Martha, feeling and understanding what it's like to have someone I loved so much taken from me for as long as this life would last. The hopes she had for her brother in this life had been destroyed, and she was trying her best to make sense of it all; and the whole story began to take on a new meaning for me. Martha wasn't faithless. She was wrestling with her faith and trying to reconcile her feelings with that faith.

I could feel every ounce of that struggle in my own heart and soul as Jeff and I sat there in that room. I felt stung and challenged by Jesus' question, "Do you believe this?" Did I *really* believe in the resurrection of the dead? Then why was I feeling the way I was? I felt guilty about feeling that way, feeling so hopeless and living in such pain at not seeing my daughter alive.

The feelings of loss at this point were overwhelming the comfort that Jeff was trying to bring me by way of this story, just as Mary's sorrow was conflicting with what she knew intellectually to be true. I wanted to share with Jeff how I perceived this conflict between my heart and my head, but the truth was that I didn't fully understand it yet myself, and that led to the guilty feelings. After further discussion with Jeff, who so patiently listened to and comforted me, the wave of grief began to recede, and I was able to get up and help Laurel, Kathleen and Roberta pick out the casket for Gayle.

When we returned home late that afternoon, we found that a neighbor had placed a wreath at the end of our driveway with the sentiment "God bless your family—from an NIU parent." Underneath the wreath in the snow were some now-frozen bouquets and plants, most of them from anonymous givers, which we tried to rescue by bringing them inside. Later, we found under the wreath a small, stuffed Huskie (Northern Illinois University's mascot) left for us by one of our neighbors who was an alumnus. Ironically, Gayle loved huskies, and often wished we owned one.

Family began to arrive over the weekend, many from out of town. Soon the house was again full of friends, neighbors and family members. In addition, the phone continued to ring off the hook. One such call was from Jocelyn McClelland. She and her husband, Stan, had lost their teenage son to gang-related violence just a few years earlier. She called to offer us their condolences, and to offer assistance when we were ready. Another was from a friend who had lost a son only three weeks earlier—whose memorial service I had just attended—calling to express his sympathies. I explained to him how every morning I cried myself awake, and I knew he understood. He encouraged me to think of my tears as a fountain overflowing in tribute to Gayle. His words helped encourage me over the days and weeks that followed.

One more benefit of having so many friends and family helping us was that we didn't have to talk directly to the newspapers or television reporters who called. Our friends shielded us from further intrusions, and we were grateful. Laurel and I finally decided we wanted to tell the world something about Gayle, and so agreed to a live interview with NBC Today, which took place on the following Monday.

Kathleen saw that her sister and I were unable to eat or talk or rest with all the people coming to see us. It must have been around seven o'clock when Kathleen gently pulled me aside and suggested that we thank everyone for coming, and tell them that we needed a break to rest and collect ourselves for what lay ahead. We needed time to be together as a family and to talk about what had happened two long days ago. She recommended that I send everyone home, and then got my permission to post a note on the front door thanking people for coming, but telling them that we would not accept any more visitors until after the funeral. So at around eight o'clock that evening I acted on her advice—after we had a prayer with our guests, people began making their way out the door, leaving Laurel, Ryan and me alone at last.

Before we retired for the night though, my sister, Liz, arrived from New York to be with us for the week of the funeral. After Laurel and Ryan visited with her for a few minutes, they went to bed, and Liz and I talked about the events of the past few days together and the plans for the days to come. Finally, by around eleven o'clock, Liz and I retired for the night as well.

In spite of wanting and needing peace and quiet, Laurel, Ryan and I still felt compelled to worship God—an expression of faith in the midst of our grief and fatigue. So, the next morning we were out the door early in the morning and off to church.

In an exhibition of the kind of lapse of attention and concentration that was typical of my mental state that morning, I discovered as I was driving that something did not feel quite right. I looked down at the floor and groaned; Laurel wondered what I was groaning about, so I pointed at my feet. Soon all of us were laughing together—I was still wearing my bedroom slippers!

While we were at church, Liz picked up our mother from the airport, and they both greeted us when we came home. Then Liz left to visit our dad and give him the attention I was not currently able to give (our parents had divorced when we were young). Some good friends came over that night to clean the house and organize things for us, which was much appreciated. Aside from family and friends—and a preliminary interview with a producer from NBC—we enjoyed a relatively peaceful Sunday.

As part of the planning for Gayle's funeral and memorial, and as outpourings of love for her and for us her family, people around the world (literally) took time to write notes—hundreds of them—on a memorial webpage that one of our church members created on the Internet website Facebook. More than that, people from as far away as Singapore sent flowers to the funeral home. Three of Gayle's cousins wrote a song for us in honor of Gayle, and recorded it for the funeral. A man who was stationed in Germany, and who used to be a member of the church in Chicago that we belong to, wrote a song about Gayle and sent us the CD; this, and another song written by a friend of Robin Weidner who had met Gayle, were posted on the Facebook page as well. Another friend, Curt Simmons, also wrote a poem for us. His poem, and two of the songs written for Gayle, were read, played or performed at her memorial service. (I will mention more about these later in the book.)

A bank account was opened in Gayle's name by another friend of ours in order to begin a scholarship, or to be used as Gayle's family thought best. Over time, thousands of dollars were contributed to that account. We decided, after considering what Gayle's wishes might be, to donate the money to a charitable group known as HOPE *worldwide*, with the principal in the account generating interest to be earmarked for youth projects funded and supported by this charity in former Soviet Union countries, where Gayle had talked about traveling and serving in orphanages.

Alyssa Julian, a neighbor girl whom Gayle taught piano, came over with her mother bringing a beautiful music box in the shape of a piano, with an older angel teaching a younger one. They asked if they could tie red and black (NIU's colors) ribbons around our trees in front of our house, and we told them they could and thanked them. Before we knew it, they had gotten permission from most of the neighbors on our street, and red and black ribbons decorated nearly every tree.

When it came time for us to tell the world about Gayle on national television, my mother really came through for us. She was there to let the camera crew in the front door at 4:30 in the morning and to help us relax before the interview. And she kept our dog, Copper, quiet in our upstairs bedroom while we spoke with the anchor over microphones and satellite television in New York City.

Finally, I was encouraged a great deal when Jeff told me that Gayle's alma mater, Glenbard North High School, had offered to let us use the school's gymnasium for Gayle's memorial service. I had no idea how many people would attend, but I was glad to know we would have the room if we needed it—and need it we did.

With all that people were doing for us, I was beginning to feel like things were well out of our hands. The clock in our living room was ticking and relentlessly chiming each hour. I wanted everything to just stop—it was all moving too fast for me. I could hardly grasp the impact of Gayle's death on our lives. I needed time to think—to reflect on what this meant to us as a family, to Laurel and me as her parents, and to me personally; but it was time I was not yet to find.

I only knew a growing awareness of things that I never got to say to Gayle—and the terrible realization that I was never able to say good-bye, never able to tell her, one more time, how much I loved her. I thought of things I never got to apologize for and things I never got to let her know I forgave her for.

In the few moments I had to think back over our last visits together, I only remembered that I could not remember the last time we had talked. Was it a week ago, two weeks ago? Why had I not called her more often? Why hadn't she called me?

I remembered the last time we saw each other. It was at a church-wide meeting at the end of January, the weekend after my being laid-off by my employer, when the church in DeKalb came to meet with the rest of the Chicagoland ministries in Northlake. I remember having trouble finding her in the crowd that morning. I was used to finding her right away whenever the DeKalb church came to town for combined meetings. She would come running up to me, and we would squeeze each other in a warm embrace, feeling how good it was to be together again. But not at this meeting. I looked for her for fifteen or twenty minutes, and when I found her, I did not feel like she was looking for me. I remember feeling let down after our brief moments together that day, and I could not figure out why. This was something that haunted me afterwards, especially after her death.

I also remembered some friction in our relationship before the holidays. She was twenty years old and growing more independent. Like most healthy young people during those college years of life, she resented her parents interfering in her decisions. Before Christmas, I believe we crossed a line with her, and she let us know it. I didn't feel like I had ever addressed that situation or apologized for it, and now it was coming back to haunt me as well. Why had she not called me as often since she went back to school?

While I wrestled inside with these thoughts, we continued to get ready for the visitation and funeral. I remember Laurel and Kathleen standing at the table in our dining room, and Laurel sharing with her sister how we had found Gayle's Bible on her bed the day after Valentine's Day. She was showing the Bible to her sister, having brought it home with her to place with Gayle's body in the casket the next day for the visitation. As they were talking about what Gayle's room looked like that morning, they happened to find something in one of the inner pockets of her Bible's case. It was a photograph taken of Gayle and me at a Valentine's Day dance for fathers and daughters when she was perhaps six or seven years old.

She is sitting on my lap wearing a pretty pink dress, her hair styled in two matching looped and braided pigtails with the sweetest smile on her face.

Laurel and Kathleen shared it with me right away, and it brought me back to life, reassuring me about her love for me. I found that though Gayle

Joe and Gayle at daddy-daughter dance, February 1992

was growing more independent, and even though she had not talked to me much in the last month, she still treasured our relationship and knew I loved her, and she loved me in return. Since that time, I cannot count the number of people with whom I have shared that picture or story. All I know is that when I needed hope and encouragement, God gave it to me through that picture.

It was this discovery that triggered my memory on the day of the visitation, the morning before the funeral, to think of a song called "The Dance," written by Tony Arata. Garth Brooks had made the song a hit a number of years earlier. Listening to the words to the song once again, I decided it would be a perfect way to end my eulogy for Gayle at the funeral the next day.

The morning of the visitation, I remembered we hadn't walked Copper since Valentine's Day morning. I thought it would be a kind thing to do for her after the chaos of the past several days. Before going outside that morning, I am vaguely certain (translation: not sure at all) I put on my glasses. I had been taking them off and putting them down to wipe tears from my eyes repeatedly the previous four days. As I mostly need them for reading and computer work, I could go for a half hour without them while talking to people around the house, by then forgetting where I was when I had taken them off. I remembered last seeing them on the dresser in our bedroom before going out. I then donned my scarf, shoes, coat and hat before putting Copper on her leash. She was so excited to be going outside for a walk, she was whimpering.

It was bitterly cold that morning. It had rained a little on Sunday, and then the temperatures dropped the following day. Overnight Monday into Tuesday morning, a light dusting of snow had fallen on the frozen streets and sidewalks, covering the ice.

I didn't foresee what was coming. I walked out of the house and down our driveway with Copper, who then bolted down the sidewalk and past a neighbor's house, with me trotting along trying to keep up. Suddenly, I saw Copper's four legs going out sideways from under her as she came upon a snow-covered patch of icy sidewalk. I remember thinking to myself, "If you can't run on four legs, how am I supposed to run on TWOOOOOOOO?"

For what felt like about five minutes, I was suspended in mid air, with my feet closer to the dog and a foot farther off the ground than my head. My hat was thrown from my head, and I came down with my full weight on my left shoulder. Wham! Fortunately, most of the air that had been in my lungs was knocked out of me by the impact, so my cry of pain was somewhat subdued. I found myself suddenly looking up at the hazy sunlit sky, attempting to coax air to return to the lungs from which it had so hastily exited, and asked God what more could happen to me that day.

Did Copper come back to check on me? No.

After lying there another minute and waiting to see if anyone had called the paramedics—no one had—I managed to roll over on to what in other seasons would have been the grass, where things were *slightly* less slippery, and pulled the dog back to where my hat also waited for me. I then made a rather unilateral decision that the walk was over, and carefully led Copper back to the safety of the house.

Upon returning to the warmth of the house, I explained to my mother and Laurel what had befallen us in our escape into the great outdoors, and asked them if they had seen my glasses. As no witness came forward to testify where they had last seen them, I went outside to retrace my steps and see if they had flown off when my hat did. After my mother and Laurel had also searched, we finally resigned ourselves to the fact that I might never find those glasses again.

After giving my attention to my missing glasses, however, I realized I had a bigger problem—I could hardly breathe. Not only had the fall knocked the wind out of me, but it felt as if the impact had dislocated or fractured a rib as well. It hurt to take a normal breath, and so physical discomfort was added to all the other pain I was feeling before the fall.

I decided then to call and try to schedule an appointment with our friend, Robbin Mitchell, who is a chiropractor. She was gracious and flexible enough to change her plans and make a house call to help us (also giving Laurel a massage for her aching neck and shoulders).

The private viewing for the family at the funeral home was scheduled to begin at 2:00 PM and last until 3:00 PM, when the public would be admitted to pay their respects to Gayle and us. This private hour went by much too quickly. I felt like I had hardly any time with Gayle, and Laurel felt the same. Nevertheless, we gave our permission to open the doors to the public and prepared for a long evening.

While we expected quite a few people to come see Gayle and to offer their sympathies to us, we were unprepared for the crowd of people who came through the funeral home that night. We could not keep up with the rate at which people showed up to see us, and within twenty minutes of opening the doors to the parlor where Gayle's body was shown, the line of people was already extending out past the door.

Three hours later, the lobby of the parlor was full of people, with friends and funeral home staff directing people to form a line that snaked back and forth throughout the lobby, and even out the front doors of the home. By 8:00, people were telling us they had waited an hour and a half to see us, some of them standing outside in the bitter cold. Still others, after seeing the line and waiting for a time, had to leave. By the funeral home's estimates, close to a thousand people came through their doors that night to see Gayle, with the last people in line not getting to us until 10:15 (the visitation was scheduled to end at 9:00).

By the time it was all over, the only way I was able to

remain on my feet when not walking was by locking my knees. Laurel stayed in the parlor greeting and talking with people the entire time, never taking a break (even to eat). My ribs and feet were very sore. Laurel had shut down all awareness of her physical condition just to get through the night. We didn't know how we would get through the following day, with the funeral planned for the morning and the public memorial service in the evening. We were, therefore, all the more grateful for the generous and loving friends who had assumed responsibility for all the plans and arrangements.

> Do you hear the people sing lost in the valley of the
>   night?
> It is the music of a people who are climbing to the
>   light...[1]

The next morning I awoke with music and the above words playing in my head. My eyes filled again with tears as I remembered the "Finale" to the musical *Les Miserables*. I lay there awake for a few minutes trying to recall the rest of the words, struggling over the next two lines for some time. I could recall the end of the song, but not the next two or three lines. Rolling over in bed, I looked at my watch and found that it was not even seven in the morning. I had slept only six-and-a-half hours, but I knew I couldn't get back to sleep.

Gayle was born around the time when *Les Miserables* first came to Chicago, and since it became my favorite musical, she grew up listening to the music from an early

---

1. "Do You Hear the People Sing" from the musical *Les Miserables,* composer Claude-Michel Schönberg with a libretto by Alain Boublil and lyrics by Herbert Kretzmer, 1980.

age. As she grew, she fell in love with the music and the story, and began insisting that we bring the tapes of the music with us whenever we went someplace in the car, and she begged to sing the songs with me as I drove. You might wonder if Laurel and Ryan tired of hearing the music over and over and over again—they did. But Gayle and I loved to sing this music as well as other Broadway musicals. Her love of music didn't end with singing to the soundtracks of her favorites, but extended to her singing and learning to play them on the piano as well.

So it was that I came to include the lyrics to a couple songs, including the "Finale" to *Les Miserables*, in the speeches I gave at her funeral and at the memorial service. It was my way of sharing our daughter's love of music with the world, and of sharing some of my fondest memories of our relationship.

The Funeral

The next morning a group of roughly ninety people gathered at the funeral home to celebrate Gayle's life and pay their final respects to her. They included extended family, Gayle's closest friends from grade school and high school, and her roommates from college. Some of Gayle's closest adult friends from DeKalb and from our church were also invited—some who had known her all her life.

The funeral began with music from the show *Wicked* (the song "For Good") and a welcome by Jeff Balsom. Then we were moved by the song that Gayle's cousins—Christian, Alisha and George—had written, performed and recorded. It was entitled "Hey Love (Gayle's Song)"—a tribute to

Gayle written to encourage her family. We were truly moved and appreciated their hard work motivated by love for us and their cousin. The lyrics celebrated her faith and her joyful spirit, and expressed their family's hope to see her again someday. (The lyrics for this song are included in the appendix.)

Following the singing of some favorite hymns and the sharing of some loving memories by our ministers, Robbin (our chiropractor friend) and her husband, Jim, shared some thoughts with the group. They had known Gayle for most of her life, and in an informal way had served in the role of godparents to our kids. But somehow, in spite of all the other wonderful remarks the two of them shared that morning, the one that stuck with me was Robbin's observation about how we were handling life the past week, and especially the previous night. She recognized how difficult the past few days had been for us, and how little time we had had to rest and to process what had happened to Gayle. Referring to the animated movie *Finding Nemo*, she quoted the little song sung by the character Dory: "Just keep swimming, just keep swimming…." This struck a chord with me. and the thought of swimming just a little further—taking things one step at a time—helped to get me through the day.

The Mitchells were followed by Gayle's aunt, Kathleen, and by friends who had known her while at school in DeKalb. All of the sharing was very heart-felt and encouraging, and made us all the more proud of Gayle and the impact her life had made on the people around her. Then, at last, it was my turn to speak and share about Gayle on behalf of her mother, brother and me:

How does one sum up over twenty years of a loved one's life in just five to seven minutes? At the best of times, it would be impossible to do—especially when that person is one's only beloved daughter. I am not going to attempt to do so this day.

Perhaps you imagine that, as a father, I feel great anger and bitterness about her death, the manner in which she died, and hate toward the crazed young man who took away her life just five days ago. Perhaps if I was a different man, I would regret sending my Gayle to NIU, regret letting her leave my constant protection. God knows the dreams that were forever shattered for her family, for her mother and brother, and for me. Dreams of her graduation from NIU. Dreams of taking her to New Zealand someday. Dreams of walking her down the aisle one day. But I am not going to spoil this opportunity to share with you about my daughter and my feelings with an angry tirade and bitter regret.

I would rather tell you about the little girl who had the cutest giggle in the whole world. Hearing her laugh was the greatest drug I could ever take. And I was addicted to it for twenty years. (I think I will be going through withdrawal—cold turkey—for a long time.) For twenty years, I reveled in making her laugh, sharing our quirky humor together; a sense of humor I inherited from my mother, her grandmother.

I want to tell you about the loving and kind spirit that she got, through me, from her grandfather Chester. I want to tell you about her sense of the importance of family, which she learned from her mother, grandparents William and Dorothy, and her aunts, uncle and many cousins. And although they never spent much time together, Gayle was remarkably like her Aunt Liz—a very quiet, privacy-loving person, who loved a good book and good music more than a crowd of people.

I want to tell you about the girl who, when she was little and playing in the back yard with friends, gave one of her girlfriends a healthy piece of her mind when she thought her little brother was being mistreated. And I have no doubt that she would go toe-to-toe with anyone twice her size if she thought there was injustice involved.

One time we were sitting in our living room when she was about four years old, watching *The Little Mermaid* (for the hundredth time), and the movie came to the end where Ariel and the prince are to be married, and I heard her say, out of nowhere, "Will you marry me, Daddy?"

I remember, more significantly, about four-and-a-half years ago, lying on the floor of her bedroom late into the night, her on her bed, while she asked me all kinds of questions about being a Christian, about Jesus and what living for him is like. She wanted to make sure that if she chose to commit her life to him, that she really meant it, and would be faithful to him all her days. And I remember baptizing her into Christ on June 6, 2004—the 22nd anniversary of the inauguration of what is now the Chicago Church of Christ. Many of you were there that day, witnesses to her confession of faith and her rebirth. To all of you: Greg and Christina Hull, Lydia Johnston, Curt and Heidi Ammons, and all the others who were so instrumental in her decision, those who led up to it, and kept her going and growing, Laurel, Ryan and I—indeed, the world—will be forever in your debt.

And for those who are looking for meaning or reassurance about why Gayle had to die at this time, I quote Isaiah 57:1–2:

"The righteous perish,
and no one takes it to heart;

the devout are taken away,
   and no one understands
that the righteous are taken away
   to be spared from evil.
Those who walk uprightly
   enter into peace, and
   they find rest as they lie in death." (TNIV)

I believe that God took Gayle home to spare her the pain and suffering that would have come to her had she stayed with us because of the evil in this world. She is in peace, sleeping and awaiting Jesus' coming.

You have probably seen the picture of Gayle sitting on my lap at a daddy-daughter Valentine's dance I took her to several through the years, and it was always the highlight of my year. Kathleen, her aunt, was looking through Gayle's Bible at our house the other day, and found tucked into the cover this picture—from about fifteen years ago. That picture will be with me the rest of my days, and let me go on record with this now—I want that picture in my casket one day.

Seeing this picture brought to mind a song that I have always liked, but never knew how apropos it would one day prove to be. I want to conclude by reading the words to this song, which so beautifully captures my feelings about this moment.

Then I quoted the words to the country song, "The Dance." It is a love song about a relationship that has ended, and the significance of that relationship to the one singing the song. It tells of how wonderful the relationship made him feel, in the words from the second verse of the song:

> Holding you [at the daddy-daughter dance in the
>   picture she had in her Bible] I held everything,

and for a moment—wasn't I the king?
If I'd only known how the king would fall, [as I did
    when I learned of Gayle's death]
Well, then who's to say, why I might have changed it
    all?[2]

I had given my heart to Gayle as her father, and now I felt all the pain of losing her. Yet somehow, in spite of how things turned out, I was grateful for the past twenty years, and that I hadn't missed the dance.

The funeral was concluded with some words of remembrance and encouragement by Chris Zillman. He shared how easy it was to come up with stories about Gayle, and how unnecessary it was to filter out anything negative about her life. Even her struggles with weaknesses ended up reflecting her character: her love for God, her pure desire to obey God with her whole heart—even when it seemed to go against her nature—and her genuine love of serving others. Then, after singing *Amazing Grace*, we were dismissed.

It was all over so fast. Like her life, it seemed to me to end so quickly.

People filed past her casket to pay their final respects as they proceeded from the room, while the song "Butterfly Kisses" played in the background. Finally the moment came when I would see Gayle's body for the last time. I stood at her side, and putting my hand on her arm, I spoke my heart to her; and in parting, I told her I loved her and said, "I will see you tomorrow," remembering that "with the Lord, a thousand years are like a day, and a day is like a thousand years" (2 Peter 3:8).

---

2. "The Dance," lyrics by Tony Arata, EMI April Music, Inc.

6

Gayle Remembered

On the night of Wednesday, February 20, 2008, we arrived at the high school by 7:00 PM and were ushered directly to our seats for the service to begin at 7:30. The parking lot was already filling with cars by then, much to our amazement. People from the community, faculty and staff of the high school and the other schools in the district where Gayle attended came out to celebrate her life and to offer their support to us. In addition, members of our church from as far away as Indiana and the Wisconsin border came to remember Gayle and to worship together. People from the university and from the DeKalb and Sycamore communities and media representatives rounded out the attendance that night.

Many people gave generously of their time and talents to make the memorial special, including a string quartet led by the mother of one of Gayle's friends and classmates from college. Floral arrangements had been brought from the funeral home and lined the stage and decorated the gymnasium. Lighting and sound were all handled by people volunteering their time and energies on our behalf. After a while, we simply sat in our seats and watched the preparations, feeling amazed and helpless.

The fact that Gayle was so suddenly taken from us was overwhelming enough. Feeling numb from the shock of her death, exhausted from the emotional energy that each hour demanded of us, bewildered at the prospect of all the change that life with only one child instead of two would mean for us, and overwhelmed by the love people were showing us and our family, we couldn't help but think that Gayle would have been dumbfounded and bewildered to see the impact her life (and death) had on the people who were coming together this night because of her.

Laurel and I looked around and talked to people who came by to offer their sympathies and encouragement, some bearing cards and some bearing gifts. As the time came for the program to begin, we simply held hands and focused on the stage, looking forward to the end of this very long week nearly as much as we were the program. Though present physically, we were incapable of fully participating in the moment; but we could see the finish line, when all this attention being showered upon us would end, and when we would have to begin facing our grief and sadness alone. We just kept swimming.

At last, the memorial program began with a welcome and a song, "Hallelujah," sung by the congregation. The song triggered memories of the four of us at home on weeknight evenings having devotionals together around our kitchen table after dinner. Laurel would pass around our songbooks, and we would take turns suggesting hymns and songs we liked to sing. Gayle began to request we sing this song sometime while she was in high school, and we would sing it together in harmony.

The words began to stick in the back of my throat as I tried to sing it with everyone else, and in the end I just stood and listened as the rest of the congregation finished the song. Given the difficulty I had trying to sing this song, I wondered how well I'd be able to hold my composure in order to say what I planned later in the evening.

The final verse of this song was especially moving that night:

> Life is but a passing glance,
> Seek Him while you have the chance:
> We are made of naught but clay,
> Till we're changed on that great day.[1]

Then we sat back and listened to story after story from people outside the family about the young woman we had raised and sent off to school, the girl we thought we knew so well.[2]

The first time I met Gayle was at a Friday night campus devotional. When the devotional was over, I was looking for some students who would be willing to come and help me clean up my apartment and hang out together. Nobody was very excited about doing this.

Then Gayle looked at me and said, "I'll do it. I'll come and help you."

"Well, Gayle," I said, "since we just met, why don't you just come over and hang out with me this time."

Well, as soon as I unlocked and opened the door, we

---

1. Music and lyrics by Geoff Fawcett. *Songs of the Kingdom* (Spring Hill, TN: DPI, 1999).

2. The stories here include some of the many that were shared during the memorial service, as well as a few that were shared with us since then. Some of the comments and stories about Gayle we heard for the first time that night.

could see into my kitchen and the big pile of dishes in the sink. Gayle goes running into the kitchen yelling "Dishes!" and just starts doing my dishes. I didn't know what to make of her, but thought, "This is awesome."

A little while later, while I'm picking up around another part of the house, she starts folding my laundry, and I think, "I'm going to become best friends with this girl." Then she gets to the big basketful of socks, and yells, "Socks!" and just starts throwing them around my living room, and I thought "Who did I bring home with me?"

"Gayle," I said, "I thought you were gonna help me clean up."

"This is how I do socks," she said. "It's like a matching game." She then proceeded to walk around my living room doing my socks.

And that's how Gayle was, always serving people. It got to a point where people would do their dishes before having her over just to keep her from doing them.

—Stephanie Sullivan

❋

Courtney, a friend of Gayle's for more than a decade, shared about her kindness and goodness and her mischievous grin: "The great thing about her was that she wasn't afraid to be herself. Even in high school, after making a lot of new friends, she remained Gayle."

It was in high school that Gayle's friends gave her the nickname "Oneichan," a Japanese word translated as "beloved older sister."

Courtney shared about Gayle's fear of and dislike for

roller coasters; about admiring Gayle's strong soprano voice; and about the many pastimes they enjoyed together. Some of these included anime, cartooning, Pokémon, Japanese pop music and the video game *Kingdom Hearts*.

In another example of Gayle's kindness and tenderheartedness, Courtney related that when war movies were

Gayle's freshman soccer picture

shown in conjunction with their history classes, and it was clear that "there'd be a lot of pain and watching people suffer, Gayle—for all her kindness—when something [painful] would come up, would reach over and cover my eyes so I wouldn't have to see what was going on, and wouldn't cry. And when the moment was over, she would whisper in my ear that it was okay."

When Gayle was home from college after her first semester, she called Courtney and asked her to meet her at the playground where they first met. There they met, hugged and talked for a long time. At that time, Gayle shared with Courtney she was "afraid of growing up, but at the same time very excited, and that she was ready to take flight." They promised each other that they would always remain friends, no matter the distance between them.

✻

Knowing how quiet and reserved Gayle was by nature, many who shared their experiences with Gayle remarked how her boldness in telling others about God challenged them. Even when her invitations were not well received by fellow students, Gayle remained undeterred. She used her courage to be herself throughout life in service for her faith as well.

❄

On another occasion, one of Gayle's friends, Michael, was escorting her home across the campus while carrying a heavy laptop in a bag while Gayle was carrying a much smaller and lighter bag. Michael began to complain about the weight of his bag on his shoulder, so Gayle offered to trade bags.

Looking at Gayle—all of five feet tall—he told her he would be fine, and continued on. But, she insisted, and so he finally gave in and traded bags with her, telling her that she probably wouldn't be able to handle it for more than a block or so. She carried it the rest of the way for him, never complaining about it once.

❄

Two of Gayle's favorite teachers, Matt Janecek and Scott Meyers, shared about Gayle. We didn't know that she had written them notes of thanks at the end of her time at Glenbard North. Her teachers shared these notes with us that night, and talked about the "lesson" that Gayle left for all of us through her life and through her letters—a lesson in the character traits of curiosity, courage, kindness, comfort and gratitude.

They observed that Gayle was imbued with a natural curiosity, an appreciation for learning as an end in itself and not merely a means to an end. They did not see her quietness as a quality of someone who was shy, but as one who was "always listening, thinking, observing and carefully crafting opinions"—and once an opinion was formed, having the courage to express and defend it.

They said that one indication that Gayle was paying attention in class was the way she would let them know she thought they'd made a mistake. According to Matt Janecek, "While some high school students might not catch you when you made a mistake, I didn't have that luxury with Gayle. I would look up at the class, and Gayle would look back at me with a slight head-cock, and the raising of a curious eye-brow, to let me know she was listening." (I laughed to myself when I heard this, as I'd received that same look myself, many times.)

They also talked about the impact of a life so short on so many people as evident from the crowd in the gym that night. (It was estimated that around two thousand people attended the memorial service.)

❄

A fellow student shared about how she loved Gayle's child-like spirit. She told about a day when snow was falling, and it looked like classes might be cancelled. Meanwhile, out into the snow runs a jubilant young woman in an off-white down-filled coat. Spreading her arms out wide, running in snow up to her knees, she tilts her head back and opens her mouth to eat fresh flakes, all the while smiling and laughing happily. Is she in grade school? No, Gayle is in college, doing what she does best—enjoying life without pretense.

Listening to these stories, I remembered Gayle asking my advice about helping a roommate with her rent the previous December. I recalled her telling me excitedly about victories she was celebrating in regard to her boldness; and I remembered her chasing her mother away from the sink at home so that she could do the dishes for her. All of these stories were so encouraging. Hearing them gave me hope that she would not be forgotten by the people whose lives she had been such a big part of for such a short time.

As the time continued, Curt Simmons read the poem he had written to Laurel and me entitled "Well Done." I had read the poem online the morning before the funeral, and I could not imagine how Curt would be able to read it without crying, as I had when I first read it; but he did. (I have included the poem in the appendix.)

Shannon Kekhaev performed the song she had written in Gayle's memory. I was struck by how it captured Gayle's joy in life and her love for music. It also expressed the sadness we felt not to hear her voice around the house anymore. (The lyrics of this song are also included in the appendix.)

When it was finally my turn to speak, I recalled many of the same memories I had shared at the funeral that morning. In addition, I made reference to the song I had requested the high school choir sing shortly before I spoke,

"Seasons of Love," from the musical *Rent*:

> Five hundred twenty-five thousand six hundred
>   minutes,
> how do you measure a year in a life?
>
> How about love?[3]

After having heard all the stories people told us that night and on many occasions since—stories of her walking across campus in all kinds of weather just to spend time with a friend, to help her with her dishes, laundry and to learn more about the Bible; the ways she gave generously to meet the needs of others even when her means to meet her own needs were small; her "spunk," her laughter, her willingness to stay up late to help roommates and friends with homework and to listen to them talk through their worries and their dreams—I see how this song was more appropriate for Gayle's memorial than I had ever appreciated before.

I concluded my remarks that night with lyrics from our favorite musical, *Les Miserables*, which I had thought about many times in the last few days. I adapted the last four lines of the song:

> Will you join in our crusade? Who will be strong and
>   stand with me?
> Somewhere beyond Cole Hall—beyond the grieving,
>   the pain, the loneliness, the rage—is there a world
>   you long to see?
> Do you hear the angels sing? Say, do you hear heaven-
>   ly choir?

---

3. "Seasons of Love." Words and music by Jonathan Larson. ©1996 Finister & Lucy Music Ltd., Co. All rights controlled and administered by EMI April Music, Inc.

It is a future of hope, and love, and peace they call us
to when tomorrow comes![4]

And Jesus and Gayle will be waiting for us there. Amen!

Chris Zillman then shared about the impact Gayle had
on him and his family, and on the DeKalb ministry overall,
reinforcing many of the same points made throughout the
service that night, and emphasizing the meaningful impact
that Gayle had made during her brief life. Soon after that,
the service was closed out with song and prayer, ending
what was another of the most memorable evenings of our
lives.

However, before we could leave to go home, we stayed
for a while to talk with those who sought us out to express
their sympathy and love. In addition, we tried to give away
most of the flower arrangements that had been used for the
funeral and memorial services, and so we found the time
approaching 11:15 before we finally left the high school.

Driving up the street toward our house minutes later,
we noticed what looked like a giant heart made of red candles in our front yard, along with the friends who were cre-
ating it in the winter's cold. Courtney and some of Gayle's
other friends had rushed to our house after the memorial
in order to set up candles in red plastic cups, buried in the
snow, to light our lawn as a surprise for us. They had trouble getting the candles to stay lit with the persistent breeze
that night, but finished the surprise just as we pulled into

---

4. "Finale" from Cameron MacKintosh's Royal Shakespeare Company Production of
the musical *Les Miserables,* composer Claude-Michel Schönberg with a libretto by Alain
Boublil and lyrics by Herbert Kretzmer. English Lyrics ©1985 Alain Boublil Music, Ltd.

our driveway. As a thank-you for her thoughtfulness, we gave one of the remaining floral arrangements (one in the shape of a heart) to Courtney.

We exchanged hugs and thank-yous, and made our way inside to find friends and family who had waited for us. After thanking them for staying at our house during the memorial and for welcoming us home, we expressed how tired we were.

Soon they were on their way, leaving us alone to think about the next stage of our lives. Though the height of the public attention was now past, and the rest of the world was about to move on, each person living their life as usual, we had no "as usual" to go back to—nor were we in any meaning of the word ready to do so. The process of grieving, for us, was just beginning.

Housechurch @ weidners
"God's Attributes"

Luke 4:16   He came to set everyone free.

Jn 4:10
    5:1-10   Interesting - he had to hear about the man's situation from other people and didn't already know.
Jesus saw the outward healing as less important than his inward healing.

    8:1-11
Romans 8:1   God created me to be free like a bird^^

Jn 9:1-8

February 14, 2008
    ➵ Valentine's Day
Psalm 141:3
       "Set a guard over my mouth, O Lord; keep watch over the door of my lips. Let not my heart be drawn to what is evil,"

Gayle's last journal entry

Part 2

After the Storm

Life is like that. It does not permit you to arrange and order it as you will. It will not permit you to escape emotion, to live by the intellect and by reason. You cannot say "I will feel so much and no more." Life, whatever else it is, is not reasonable.

—Agatha Christie in *Sad Cypress*

7

Only Hope

Following Gayle's death and her funeral, I became increasingly aware of my feelings about our relationship. I felt like I had been robbed of so many dreams and expectations—mine and hers—for what I had always assumed would be a long life. But more than that, I felt robbed of an opportunity to say so many things to her, and to find out where I stood with her in our relationship. I mentioned before that there had been some friction between us over the holidays just past, and I hadn't felt the usual closeness and warmth between us the last time we saw each other.

This led me to look forward to reading Gayle's final journal, the one we found on her bed at school, to see if I could find any clues to how *she* was feeling about me and our relationship in the last month or two of her life. Laurel had already begun reading it during the week after Valentine's Day and had shared with me some of the things she found, but they were more about Gayle and her relationship with and feelings toward God than about her relationship with us, her parents. And so I was interested in looking at the journal for my own satisfaction, to find what would comfort *me*.

What I found was not what I was looking for; instead I found in her journal the notes and prayers of a young woman who looked at God as her only hope, her one guiding passion. Several times a week—sometimes daily—she would sit and write down her prayer (a letter) to God for the day. Her prayers were informal and from the heart. If she was disappointed in herself or indignant about some sin in her life, she told God about it; if she was in awe of the way she saw God working in her life or in the church, she shared her feelings with God. Day after day she prayed for friends at school, for her childhood friends back home, for her roommates, for the work of the church in DeKalb,

Gayle, dressed in over-alls—her favorite clothing—while serving Appalachia Service Project in Harlan County, KY (2006)

and for her family (especially for her brother, Ryan, who got the most mention of any family member).

She asked God for help with overcoming temptations and weaknesses, and for forgiveness for specific sins. But above all things, what stood out was her joy in following Jesus and her heart's desire to have an impact on the world for God.

The following pages contain direct quotes from Gayle's final two journals, featuring entries from the last few months of her life. The punctuation, grammar, spelling and style are hers, and along with her words reflect her personality.[1]

November 18, 2007
  Bethany's baptism & physical b-day

  God, thank you so much for this day and that Bethany is getting baptized. God, I pray for her, that

---

1. Omissions have been made of some names for the sake of privacy. In some such cases, I have included a blank or only an initial of the person she is writing (or praying) about.

you continue to teach her your ways and help me to be a good example for her. God, I pray that you'd open the hearts of all the people who are studying the Bible, God, that they'll want to have a relationship with you and really see their sin. Please help me to reach out to people and to ask them to study the Bible and come to church. Please lead me to those whose hearts are ripe for the picking. God, I love how you put us in the right place at the right time and that you are in control… Please show me what you want me to do with my life and that I can be happy with it no matter if I don't get to travel or not…God, you are awesome and so worthy of our praise every single day of our lives. I pray that I can worship you acceptably from the heart today. I love you. It's in Jesus' name I pray. Amen.

December 12, 2007
  Psalm 8

  "O Lord, our Lord,
  how majestic is your name in all the earth!
  You have set your glory above the heavens.
  From the lips of children and infants you have ordained praise because of your enemies,
  to silence the foe and the avenger.
  When I consider your heavens, the work of your fingers…
  the moon and the stars, which you have set in place,
  what is man that you are mindful of him,
  the son of man that you care for him?
  You made him a little lower than the heavenly beings and crowned him with glory and honor.
  You made him ruler over the works of your hands;

you put everything under his feet:
all flocks and herds, and the beasts of the field,
the birds of the air, and the fish of the sea,
all that swim the paths of the seas.
O Lord, our Lord, how majestic is your name in all the
earth!"

God, this is so true. You deserve our praise and all the glory… You've given us everything we need to live in this world. You remember that I'm dust and you're exceedingly gentle with me. You know what I can and cannot handle and you know my heart. God, thank you so much for giving us authority over everything you've created and more. You're awesome and you are so unpredictable, God. Thank you for being who you are and for wanting a relationship with me. Thank you so much for Jesus and the Bible and the Cross. Thank you so much for the Holy Spirit and for your Grace. Thank you for being patient and merciful when I mess things up. God, nothing is impossible for you…Please help me to surrender to your will for my life—that I can be happy and filled with joy no matter what I end up doing. God, I have so many walls up when I get together with _____. …

God, I pray that you'd help me to get a job soon so I can fill the hole in my bank account and so it'll be one less thing I have to worry about—even though I shouldn't be worrying if I trust you and have faith that you'll take care of me… Anyway, God, I helped [?] knowing that you wouldn't leave me hanging… Please help me to be patient and to be wise… You will take care of me. I have to believe that. God, I also pray that we can find a townhouse as cheap as this next year that we can all be pleased with—that it'll have a garbage disposal and washer/dryer/dishwasher that'll work…or that we can stay here next year. I pray for ____…that she'll want to know you, God. I also pray for finals, God, that everybody will do awesomely and that I can study well and bring my GPA up. I also pray that my Astronomy teacher'll pass me so I won't have to take it again… I love you. It's in Jesus' name I pray. Amen.

December 19, 2007
→ job hunting

Psalm 18:30
"As for God, his way is perfect; the word of the Lord is flawless.
He is a shield for all who take refuge in him.
For who is God besides the Lord?
And who is the Rock except our God?
It is God who arms me with strength and makes my way perfect.
He makes my feet like the feet of a deer; he enables me to stand on the heights."

God, if it is your will, please help me to get a job during break… I want to be surrendered to your will in everything… I have no idea what I'm doing or what I'm in DeKalb to do…but I want to please you. I don't know how to open up to people and mentor them or talk about my life with them… Oh! God, I pray that Stephanie's delivery will go smoothly and that the baby will come on time and that I can help her take care of it… Please be with her and the baby—that they'll both be healthy afterwards. Thank you for her willingness to disciple me… It's in Jesus name I pray. Amen.

Gayle wrote the following entries while she was home for Christmas break.

December 23, 2007
  Psalm 27:1

"The Lord is my light and my salvation—whom shall I fear?
The Lord is the stronghold of my life—of whom shall I be afraid?"

God, thank you for this day and that we get to wor-ship you today and remember what Jesus did for us. God, I pray that we can please you with our hearts and eagerness to praise you. I want to make you smile and be proud of me. Thank you so much for this hol-iday that I was able to see C____ yesterday. Thank you for the townhouse and my roommates. Thank you for the DeKalb church, God. And the ministry…God, I want to do awesome things there for you… I want to do what I was called to do. Please use me somehow… and make me into an awesome Christian that gets persecuted for you more than anyone else… Thank you so much for Jesus and the Cross. I love you. It's in Jesus' name I pray. Amen.

January 14, 2008
→ Classes start

God, thank you for this day, and for getting us up this morning to pray and get ready for the semester. God, please change my heart so I can reach out to people today and to not want to keep to myself because of the cold…cuz right now all I want to do is get warm and stay that way. Please help me to love people and to look for the good qualities in each person rather

than the bad and to do your will with a cheerful atti-
tude. Please humble me and show me the ways I need
to change even more… I want to be like Jesus, God. I
made the decision four years ago and now I need to
do the things you've called me to do. Thank you so
much for being who you are and for giving us Jesus
and hope of salvation… Thank you for loving me so
deeply even though I know I don't deserve any of it.
Thank you so much for my family and the people
you've put in m[y] life. Thank you for the comfort
you offer and the grace you've showed. Thank you so
much for providing for me to be here and come to
school here. I'm here for a reason, God. I pray that I'll
do what you've put me here to do and not leave until
I've done it. I pray that me and Ionela will find some
open people who truly do want to seek you and
understand how to be saved. Please make us bold and
help us to overcome the things we fear and to have
faith instead of anxiety—that we can accomplish
awesome, huge things this semester—things that we
can tell the next generation about…and bring glory
to you, Lord. God, I need you so much…please speak
through me and let everything I say come from your
Spirit, God. It's in Jesus' name I pray, Amen.

During the last weeks of January and first weeks of
February, Gayle was trying to find a way to contribute a gift
to the care package her friends were putting together for
Brad Procek, a young man who had accepted an internship
with the church in Jerusalem. She wanted to send him a
slingshot. To Gayle, Brad was like Israel's King David as a
young man, and she thought the best gift to send him was
one reminiscent of the weapon David used to slay giant

Goliath. Her friends had reservations about whether such a gift would ever make it through customs.

29 January, 2008
→ *BT @ 8 pm*

> God, I pray for the girls I reached out to yesterday, that they will be sincerely interested and that they'll come check it out tonight and they'll like it. I pray that I can be [a classmate]'s friend and stick with her, even if she doesn't want to talk with me or Ioni about the Bible. I pray that you'd work on her heart to want to come to Bible Talk or church with us. Please help her to overcome her fear of Christians. We are hypocrites—but we are trying to live by the Bible… right? God, I want to baptize someone this semester—and study the Bible with them… Please give me wisdom to lead people and be responsible…make me ready—cuz I'm a little scared of leading. If I'm wrong about something, then everyone knows about it… Do I be humble and say 'Oops' or what? Please teach me…and help me to be friends with those girls in Anthropology and that you'll open their hearts to be willing to learn about the Bible. Please help me to know what to say and how to say it and when to say it. I do care…I remember how I was when I was just going to church.[2] It was so empty…and lonely… God, thank you so much for saving me from that darkness and fear of dying… Thank you for Jesus and the things he had to go through so I could be with you like he was. It's in Jesus' Name I pray. Amen.

---

2. Here she was referring to the time while she was growing up, before she was baptized after deciding to follow Jesus as Christ, her Lord.

February 6, 2008
→ *Snow Day! No School!*
→ *[Prayer time] w/ Stephanie @ 2?*
→ *Mdwk*

> *God, thank you so much for answering our prayers and for giving us a lot of snow so school closed. I wonder what I'm gonna do today… God, I don't want to be who I am right now… I want to be who you meant me to be…when will I get there? I feel like so many people are going to stay lost if I don't change real soon… God, I want to be used by you… I don't want to let the campus ministry down—or the church. I want to do big things… but… who would I do them for? That's just the thing, though… I want to do things so others can see them… and acknowledge that I did them. God, I'm so weak right now… please forgive me for thinking and feeling these things and for caring more about the praise I get from people rather than you. God, please help me to be content with what you give me and the praise I'll receive from you one day. God, thank you so much for everything you've done in my life and for listening to my prayers. It's in Jesus' Name I pray. Amen.*

During one of her prayer times with her friend Stephanie, Gayle confided in her that she wanted to do great things for God and have an impact on others for him. She did not feel like her life was making a difference on people and on the world around her. She felt insecure and didn't think she amounted to much. At her memorial service, Stephanie shared how she was taken aback by Gayle's confession, and how she tried to encourage Gayle with the fact that she *was* having an impact on people already, even when she did not realize it or see it.

On February 8, Gayle and I shared our last phone call. During the call, we talked about her grandfather's health and about my search for work. We also talked briefly about her new major. Aside from that, it hurt to say, I couldn't remember what else we said to each other. We always assumed there would be more calls, more conversations. Looking back, I wished we had talked on the phone more often, but Gayle was striving to be more independent and responsible, and her mother and I respected her need to learn to stand on her own feet. Fostering and respecting that independence I don't regret; I only regret what we didn't (couldn't) know what was about to happen.

Gayle began planning and working with her friends to prepare the Valentine's Day dinner around this time. She also went on what would be her last date.

February 11, 2008

> God, thank you for this day. Thank you that I get to come to you and know that you're listening. Thank you for this townhouse and my roommates. Thank you for the campus ministry and for all the people who are studying the Bible. God, I pray for ___, that her heart will be moved by the Scriptures…I pray for all the other people that you'd be with them and help them each to come to decisions of their own accord. God, please help me to be fruitful and to be excited about Bible Talks and the mission we've been given…that I can share my faith with people. Please give me courage and strength, God…cuz I don't feel like I can be used… I'm not outgoing… I don't have the personality all the others have. God, please open my mouth… Thank you so much for your mercy and

patience and for giving me a purpose—that I have a reason to live… It's in Jesus' Name I pray. Amen.

February 12, 2008
→ Bible Talk @ 8 pm

February 13, 2008
→ Housechurch
→ Dtime with Stephanie @ 2
   Psalm 119:08

"Accept, O Lord, the willing praise of my mouth, and teach me your laws. Though I constantly take my life in my hands, I will not forget your law."

The above was followed by her final entries, which I shared with you in the first chapter.

After reading Gayle's journals, I remembered my friend's words to me the night we found and identified her body in Rockford, "Brother, your work is finished." Laurel and I had passed down to our daughter the faith and love that we had for God—modeled imperfectly, but honestly and consistently. Few things could have provided me with a greater reward than knowing that, in the words of songwriter Mark Schultz, "She was watching." She had developed her own faith, her own convictions, and lived them out after she left home.

Nevertheless, I felt an incompleteness in my heart because of the many things I wished I could have told her and could have done for her, but now—thanks to the evil acts of a young man—would never enjoy.

8

Letters to Gayle

Coming down the stairs to the kitchen the morning after the funeral, I was numb. Walking into the dining room I saw papers, file folders, brochures on assisted living facilities (that I had been comparing for my father to move into), and books that had been dumped against the far wall as if the room had been hit by a tsunami. These remnants of my life had been swept aside by Gayle's death and the waves of people who had come through the house over the past week, leaving in their wake platters of food on the tables.

In between the plates of food were plants and flowers. The plants were the overflow of the veritable garden in the living room—some of them from the funeral, others gifts from people who brought them to us the Friday and Saturday before. Some of the plants had been left on our porch or by the wreath on the snow bank outside, and were already showing signs that they would not survive. There was hardly a horizontal surface in the house that wasn't covered with plants, flowers, photographs or food.

In the family room, poster boards that carried pictures from various periods of Gayle's life were placed alongside the wall and in front of the fireplace, along with more flowers, baskets of cards, and cases of soft drinks and bottled water. In all, there was not a single place where one could sit down and not be reminded that this was a home that had borne the impact of tragedy. Every place I looked, everywhere I turned, I was reminded that Gayle was gone. There was no reminder of peace, nowhere to escape, nowhere to forget.

And, if that wasn't difficult enough for me to deal with, the fact that it was Laurel's birthday made it even more difficult for *her*. There would be no "happy birthdays" for Laurel on this birthday; somehow "happy birthday" didn't seem appropriate, or remotely possible.

The doorbell rang around 8:30 that morning—it was Roberta Balsom, who had come to deliver some fresh baked scones for our breakfast. I asked her if she would like to stay and have one with us, but she declined, saying she just wanted to make sure we were cared for, and to wish Laurel the best birthday she could have under the circumstances. Following a quiet breakfast with Laurel, Ryan and my mother, I decided to venture out to buy a replacement for the eye glasses I lost and to find some gift to lift Laurel's spirits.

My first trip to a store by myself since Gayle's death was a strange experience for me. It was the first time in over a week when I wasn't in the company of people who knew who I was, or what I had been through. It being the day after Gayle's funeral, even people who had felt some measure of loss in her death were getting back to their jobs, their schools and their errands. For our family, our adjustment and mourning period was only beginning. And for me, I didn't have much to go back to—no job, no school, no routine—only a houseful of memories and mementos and clutter. I felt lost.

An hour and a half later, I had a gift for Laurel (a book of devotional readings by author Max Lucado) in which I wrote something personal to her and *two* pairs of glasses (I bought some sunglasses, too). In leaving the shopping mall I discovered that I not only felt lost, but *was* lost; I couldn't find my car. I started walking around in the cold parking lot, going down each row, trying earnestly to find the place where I had parked.

Eventually, I called home and explained my predicament to Laurel. I assured her I would eventually find it, and then hung up. Soon after that, I did find the car. However, the experience left me with doubts about myself and my ability to take care of myself and my family in the state of mind I was in.

The day after the shooting occurred at the university, we had received a call from a man named Steve Lux. He introduced himself as Gayle's teacher for her freshman orientation class, and told us she had made a big impression on him as a student. So, when he heard of her death, he volunteered to serve our family as liaison to NIU and see that our needs were met by the university. We were delighted to hear that someone with a personal connection to Gayle at NIU wanted to help us navigate any bureaucracy that might delay the university meeting whatever needs we might have.

During the course of the week following the shooting, Steve was in touch with us nearly every day by phone; he came and introduced himself to us in person at Gayle's visitation, and was there the night of the memorial service at

Glenbard North. He kept us informed about the events the university was planning.

The university closed, suspending classes following the shooting, and classes hadn't resumed yet. Students had gone home, and the university temporarily suspended normal operations in order to allow students, parents and faculty a chance to mourn and grieve, and to assess what to do in order to return to normal again. Virginia Tech, having suffered a similar tragedy only ten months earlier, served as an advisor and model to NIU for meeting the needs of all affected by the shooting in DeKalb.

As part of the healing process, the university administration and faculty decided to hold a memorial service for the victims and to recognize the wounded. It was to be a rallying point for the school to unite and stand together as "Huskies," and encourage students and faculty to return to work and class. In addition, the students and faculty would be told about some of the measures taken and services provided by the university during the following week to help people adjust to their return to classes and to work.

When we received an invitation to the event, we made plans to attend. We let Ryan choose whether or not he wanted to attend, and he opted not to.

After church on Sunday, we had lunch at the Weidners' house. Friends shared a number of stories from the past week with us, but the one that stood out to me was about the candlelight vigil the night after the shooting. On that occasion, a twenty-minute vigil was held on the commons area near Cole Hall, and at the moment when the vigil began it started to snow; when the ceremony was over, the snow stopped. Someone shared that they felt like Gayle was sending us a sign to let us know she was all right.

After lunch, we returned to the townhouse with Gayle's roommates and went once more to her room. I took pictures of the room, wanting to preserve it as it was, as close as possible to the way she had left it that fateful morning. We found a few more things that we wanted to bring home with us, and we asked the girls when they would like us to bring the rest of Gayle's belongings home (we wondered if leaving her things there would help them adjust). We told them they could keep things the way they were for the rest of the school year if it would help them. They told us there was no reason to rush or delay the move for their sake, and so we decided to wait until the semester was finished and we could get some help from the family with the move.

As we were concluding our visit, a thought occurred to me. I went to Gayle's CD/cassette player, and out of curiosity, pressed the eject button to find out what the last tape was that Gayle ever played. When it slowly opened, I saw our copy of *Les Miserables*.

Steve Lux met us at the rendezvous point for transporting us to the memorial and introduced us to the families of the other students who had been slain. After offering our sympathies to one another, the bus chartered for us by the university took us to the Convocation Center on NIU's campus.

Along the way to the school, Steve handed us a brown paper sack. He told us that it was what the police had been able to identify as Gayle's from the crime scene. Up to this point, we had not received even a trace of Gayle's clothing—

not a coat nor a backpack, not a shoe nor a purse. In the bag we found:

* A spiral notebook with "Anthropology" written on the cover, and a few pages filled in with class notes.
* A folder for the same class, which preceded the oceanography class.
* A small pocket stapler
* A crumpled $20 bill
* A nail clipper
* A pocket-sized, leather bound black Bible (New International Version, heavily underlined, with notes in the back)
* In a smaller bag labeled "L-18" was her cell phone (with a little butterfly sticker on it).

We wept as we looked at these last belongings. Steve told us that anything else that Gayle had with her in the class had been disposed of, having been ruined in the shooting or lost. We believe that included a backpack, a red shoulder bag that was given her by a friend, her books from her last classes, and the clothing she was wearing that day. We were deeply disappointed to have so little returned to us, but understood the circumstances would not allow it to be any different.

Steve also presented us with an envelope containing some papers of Gayle's he had kept after her semester as one of his students. For him to have saved her work after the class was over showed us how unique and special she was to him. Many times he cried with us, that night and since, thinking of her death.

Beginning a few nights after her death, after the crowds had dissipated and we were alone in our house for the first time, I began a ritual of going into Gayle's bedroom at night and sitting on the edge of her bed with a photo I had found of her, and talking to her before retiring for the night. I would tell her about my day, about all that people had told us about her, and about the impact that her death had had on people. I would confess how much I missed her and wished she was really there with me. Sometimes I would read a passage from the Bible to her picture, and other times I would simply sit on her bed and read silently from a book that we both enjoyed while she was living.

The truth was that I was *not* finished with Gayle. Though the physical aspect of our relationship was over, the emotional and spiritual aspects lived on. I continually labored under the weight of intense grief over all the things that I wanted to say to someone who was no longer there. I wanted to reach out to her for one more hug, call her on the phone and hear her laugh one more time, listen to her sing one more song—only to be denied. The denial was permanent; the feelings would not go away.

Easing my grief became my primary need, and doing so occupied much of my time and attention when I was not taking care of Laurel and Ryan, or looking after my father. Waking up on Monday morning following the memorial ceremonies at NIU, I remembered the crosses that I had seen in the video at the memorial the night before—crosses that someone had built, painted and placed on the hill overlooking the clearing between Cole Hall and the student center. Each of the five crosses bore the name of one of the victims of the shooting, and the video showed students placing candles and flowers in front of the crosses during the week

Memorial cross for Gayle on the NIU campus

after the shooting. I suddenly felt a need to visit the site and place my own flowers there. That became my first order of business the week after the funeral.

Thinking that I would feel better after I did, I decided to make the trip that Monday morning. I asked Laurel if she wanted to go back to DeKalb with me. She declined, too exhausted from the past ten days to think of venturing out of the house and sitting in a car for another long ride. So, stopping at a florist along the way, I made my way back to NIU and to the hill where the crosses stood.

Bouquet in hand, I walked to the end of the walk that ran along the hill where the crosses were placed. Gayle's cross was on the far right of the row of crosses. In front of and all around the crosses were piled tokens of remembrance and love, so much so that the snow was completely covered around the crosses. The hill wasn't terribly high or steep, but the snow was covered with a layer of ice (it was raining lightly at the time), and so the footing was treacherous. I carefully picked my way up the hill, negotiated my way through all the other gifts that had been laid around her cross, and reaching the top, I bent over and gently placed my bouquet up against it, saying softly "I love you." I placed the card I'd written inside the wrapping to ensure it wouldn't be spoiled by the weather.[1]

Once finished on the hill, I walked past the parking lot where less than two weeks earlier I had seen on television the emergency vehicles and students being carried to awaiting ambulances, and went to see Cole Hall. I crossed the bridge and approached the hall, trying to imagine how it looked to Gayle on the day of her last class. The building was locked and sealed with crime scene tape. Against the outside wall of the building, more flowers and candles were laid, and notes were written remembering the names of the fallen. I thought it looked like such an ordinary, even insignificant building—now one with eternal significance to me.

In the end, I felt relieved I had made the trip. I didn't feel right not going through the motions that so many strangers had done in remembrance of Gayle (and the other victims). And like so many people who visit the graves of their loved ones, I was looking for relief from the pain caused by remembering what was and could never be again, things that would forever remain unsaid, and the expectations—for her life and ours—that had been shattered. On that bitter hill I felt peace, if only for a moment. But grief remained, adding pain to Gayle's memory and making my heart its home.

---

1. On a visit a couple weeks later, Laurel and Ryan visited this hill with me, Laurel placing her own bouquet next to the cross. Ryan presented Gayle with his own personal gift: a brand new set of prized drumsticks.

Though not being one to regularly keep a journal, I began to keep one starting with the week following the shooting. My first journal entry after Gayle died was on the 22nd of February, when I quoted Proverbs 22:1: "A good name is more desirable than great riches, to be esteemed is better than silver and gold."

In meditating on all that had been done on behalf of our family and in remembrance of Gayle over the previous week, I wrote:

> *The value of the esteem and good name has come from God, and far outweighs the silver and gold of the U.S. Treasury. All of it. I have always been proud of my daughter. Now that I see her life from beginning to end, I am more proud of her than ever.*

I was deeply moved by the love and support we had received since we learned of the shooting at NIU and felt a great indebtedness to many people.

Five days later, inspired by Gayle's written prayers, I wrote the following prayer (a profound description of grief):

> *Lord, I feel weak and fatigued; I am an old man in a*
> * worthless body.*
> *I go to sleep at night, too tired to toss and turn; yet in*
> * my sleep I find no rest.*
> *Though I lay my head down at midnight with no alarm*
> * to awaken me,*
> *my grief is my alarm, and with tears I wash my face*
> * before dawn's light.*
> *I think of Gayle's tiny soft hands, her loving embrace,*
> *and how empty I feel without her understanding and*
> * companionship.*

*My mind freezes and anger wells up within me—anger
    at her attacker, despair that I am not there to defend
    her—deepest of anguish I could not be the last voice
    she heard, and could not hold her till she was asleep.*
*Then, had I not saved her, I could have asked to join
    her in her sleep,*
rest alongside her and wait [the coming of] our God.
*I cannot bear to picture the scene, her last moments, be
    a witness to the fear she felt, the terror of that gun
    man;*
*to do so is more than I can handle, and I ask God to
    please deaden in me the power of my imagination.*

*Lord, I believe in your mercy, and I seek comfort and
    take comfort in your refuge.*
*I believe Gayle finished her race and knows the peace
    you promise.*
*I have read her journals, her prayer requests, and in
    them heard her inmost thoughts—*
things she shared with none but you.
*And I believe she is with you, that you will and have
    defended her from her accuser.*
*I believe you are honoring her as one honors soldiers of
    great valor, as one esteems those who show kindness
    to the poor.*
*In this I take comfort: that you keep all your promises;
    that you are the way, the truth, and the life, and that
    by you Gayle has found her way home.*

I humbly ask your strength and comfort;
please help me find my breath.
Please help me find my way to you as well,
to finish my race strong and true.
May I find shelter in you, oh God,

and mercy along my way.
And may your grace to me overflow to others
that together with me we can join Gayle at your side.
Amen

A week later, I wrote:

Been difficult to concentrate on things the past five days
while suffering with the flu. Today is the first day I have
been without a fever since Friday night. But, with the
return of my health has come a return of grief. I had a
number of painful episodes, thinking of things I wish I
had said, but did not, and vice versa.

Still aching to finish all I had to say to Gayle, but which
she wouldn't have a chance to hear, I took the advice of a
friend and bought a separate journal—a spiral bound notebook in which to write my "letters to Gayle" and to serve as
a keepsake for generations to come. My first entry, dated
March 8, began…

Dearest Gayle,

It may have been, I believe, four weeks ago today
when last we spoke over the phone. Today I cannot call
you, except in my heart. So I will begin to write to you
instead.

Actually, I have written to you already, in my other
journal, one I began using just a couple weeks before
you left us. I just bought this journal to write to you, as
a gift for you, hoping that somehow the love I convey
herein will somehow be communicated to you wherev-
er this finds you, wherever God has you in his arms.

I go on in my letters to Gayle to talk about memories we
shared when she was alive, such as the last Christmas present

I bought her: a collection of DVDs containing a half-dozen A&E romance movies, which I planned to give her one at a time over the course of a few years, but only had a chance to give her the first one before her death. I recounted how happy I was to see her enjoying it, and how much I regretted that she missed the movies I wouldn't be able to give her now. A visit to Costco earlier in the day led to the memory about the movies and triggered a wave of regret that drained the enjoyment out of my shopping trip.

I expressed relief that she hadn't survived the shooting only to be crippled or disfigured the rest of her life. I wrote that I was happy that she was spared a life-time of memories of the shooting, fear of sudden noises and of people sneaking up on her, of jumping when doors opened suddenly, and of guilt, wondering why she lived and others died. I went on in great detail about all these thoughts and more.

In later entries, I recounted the sequence of events on the day of the shooting from our perspective, looking for forgiveness for taking so long to drive out to DeKalb in response to the shooting. I also told her how proud I was of her, of the way she lived out her faith, of the way she denied herself to be her best for God. In all of this, I was looking to complete that which was left unfinished in our relationship. In the end, however, I still had days in which I felt little energy for life, and when I felt unexpected waves of fatigue and remorse, minutes and hours where all I felt like doing was staring out into space, not thinking of anything in particular.

On May 17, the university honored Gayle with a diploma from the College of Liberal Arts and Sciences in anthropology.

Laurel, Ryan and I walked across the stage of the Convocation Center to receive the honorary diploma when Gayle's name was announced, and a standing ovation was given as her picture was displayed on the jumbotron in the middle of the amphitheater. It was one of the most bitter-sweet moments of my life.

Following the receipt of the diploma, we picked up the rest of Gayle's belongings from the townhouse. Laurel and I gave the other family members a brief tour of the main and downstairs levels of the house, this being the first time they had been there. As we passed through the living room and the kitchen, we made mental note of the things that belonged to Gayle and that we wanted to take with us: a few DVDs and VHS tapes that either belonged to Gayle or to our family library, a pretty blue candle holder and a few other ornaments, a set of glasses that Laurel had given Gayle to help furnish the apartment, and a small assort-ment of other dishes.

We had packed most of her belongings during an earli-er visit, so I took the boxes we brought with us and began filling them with the remaining odds and ends and disman-tled her computer desk. Everyone pitched in, and in about an hour, everything belonging to Gayle had been carried outside. After the last item had been removed, and while the family decided which things would fit best in whose vehicle, I stood alone in the empty room, listening to the walls and wanting them to tell me a story—a story of Gayle.

I listened to the silence of the desolate room with its bare walls, unadorned window ledge, and vacant closet. I tried to hear the least echo of her voice reverberating through the house. I tried to imagine how it sounded with her singing at the top of her lungs. I thought of her and Claudia talking to each other down the hall at night, or of her yelling good-bye to roommates as they left for work or classes. I wanted the walls to speak to me, and I listened.

I remembered seeing the room in this state only five and a half months earlier and helping Gayle plan where she wanted us to set everything. I remembered her thrill and excitement at having her own room, a place to call her own. I remember seeing it and thinking, "Gee, this is small." She looked at it and thought, "Home, sweet home." I remembered returning to DeKalb the day after she first moved in, bringing her house-warming presents of a mat for her desk chair to roll on, an indoor/outdoor thermometer so she would know how cold it was outside and how to dress, and some desk organizers—and her bicycle.

Joe and Gayle on Maid of the Mist at Niagara Falls, June 2005

I thought about her calling me at work to tell me that her computer monitor was dead, only to find out that the power plug had jiggled loose from the back of it. I thought of her decision to stop watching anime on YouTube because she wasn't getting any work done. I tried to imagine her sitting at her desk late into the night watching some Japanese animated romance or adventure story, then getting mad at herself when she realized that she had stayed up so late and had a test later that morning.

I imagined her sitting on her bed the morning of 2/14, just three months earlier, reading Psalm 141 and writing a hurried note in her journal before running off to class. I thought about how these walls had seen her gather her books, put them in her backpack along with her Bible and a little cash for emergencies, and with hardly a thought or a second look, walk out the door of her home for the last time. If she had any premonition that morning, we will never know. If only walls could talk. I glanced around one last time at the walls, took a couple more deep breaths, wiped my eyes, and said good-bye.

While writing letters to Gayle provided temporary relief for my grief, writing in general helped me to think more clearly about my feelings and my situation at a time when clear thinking was most difficult. I had lived through the loss of my livelihood and my daughter all in the span of less than a month, and was witnessing the slow death of my father as week by week I took him to doctor after doctor, surgery after surgery (he finally died on June 11, just four months after Gayle).

Around the time of the graduation, I described to a friend my feeling like "I'm on a vessel on a stormy sea, with no sign of land, and an anchor that won't hold. The skies are cloudy, and I can't find my bearings by sun or stars. When I do see land, it's far away, and I don't recognize it. When I try to steer a course toward it, I find it is no longer there; I must be sailing in circles."

To my mother I described walking around my house like "walking through a battlefield and getting hit with shrapnel; everywhere I turn there I'm hit by visions of plants, flowers, sympathy cards, pictures of Gayle, piles of papers that used to be my work but now mean nothing to me. Home isn't a refuge; it is a constant reminder of what I've lost."

I was used to, for most of twenty-five years, getting up and going to work early in the morning, Monday through Friday, spending evenings and weekends taking the kids to their sporting or music activities, going to church, etc. I had a routine. I had people depending on my being places at set times and working on specific projects. I was very project-driven. Suddenly, I was without projects, without deadlines, without a place to go or anyone expecting me to go there.

I decided that I needed to get out of the house on a regular basis, even if it was just to sip coffee, to read, to look for work (though most companies wanted me to apply via the Internet), and have someplace to go—a reason to get dressed every day.

I read a statistic years ago that I remembered at this time: Bereaved parents are much more likely to divorce than parents who haven't lost children. Remembering this fact put me on my guard, and as a result, I fostered a safe haven in our household where Laurel and I could openly share our feelings with one another, free of judgment and criticism, and without either of us trying to "fix" the other or solve their problems. We found that though we had both lost the same daughter, our feelings were very different, as were the ways we dealt with those feelings. With the great jumble of conflicting feelings I had inside, I often had to write them down in order to understand them myself; I sometimes shared what I wrote with Laurel, who read them with amazing compassion and respect, and together we labored to understand each other better.

Of all the writing I did during these months after Gayle's death—letters to Gayle, prayers and journal entries—the journal entries helping me understand my grief proved to be the most beneficial, paving the way for recovery from my losses.

9

Not Our Plans

I had a hard time in the weeks following the funeral deciding what to study in the Bible. Often I would open to Psalms and just start reading. I also found that I related to Jeremiah's Lamentations more than in the past. In Lamentations 3:1–3, Jeremiah described the way I felt as he spoke for himself:

> I am the man who has seen affliction
> by the rod of his wrath.
> He has driven me away and made me walk
> in darkness rather than light;
> indeed, he has turned his hand against me
> again and again, all day long.

Day after day, I felt deserted by God. All day long I felt like I was walking under a cloud, or like I was carrying bags of rocks around my neck. I woke up tired with sorrow, and each night I retired exhausted as if from great toil—even if all I'd done was run a few errands. Yet, in my heart, I didn't feel the condemnation of God, and so I waited for him as did Jeremiah:

> Because of the LORD's great love we are not con-
> demned,
> for his compassions never fail.
> They are new every morning;
> great is your faithfulness.

I say to myself, "The LORD is my portion;
    therefore, I will wait for him."
The LORD is good to those whose hope is in him,
    to the one who seeks him;
it is good to wait quietly
    for the salvation of the LORD. (Lamentations
3:22–26)

But the question remained, as I waited for him to answer, "Where was God on the afternoon Gayle and her classmates were killed?"

Toward the end of June, shortly after my father's death, I picked up and began reading a chapter in the book *Suffering and the Sovereignty of God,* which had been given to us by a friend. In the chapter entitled "Sovereignty, Suffering, and the Work of Missions" by Stephen F. Saint, I found the personal account of a missionary whose father had been killed by the people he was reaching out to, and whose own daughter, Stephanie, died suddenly (at about the same age as Gayle had).[1]

I felt a kinship to the author as he shared his feelings about his only daughter. He remembered not wanting to accept the fact that Stephanie was growing up, and he had felt the pain—as I had—of sending his daughter off to college. His daughter also played piano, as did Gayle, and enjoyed seeing the world and playing music as part of a Youth for Christ world missionary tour (Gayle wanted to serve in orphanages in Russia and Ukraine someday). But

---

1. Stephen F. Saint, "Sovereignty, Suffering, and the Work of Missions" in *Suffering and the Sovereignty of God,* John Piper and Justin Taylor, editors (Wheaton, IL: Crossway Books, 2006), 119.

upon returning home from her world tour, she was stricken at her home with a massive cerebral hemorrhage.

Sharing about rushing to the hospital to be with her, Saint muses "Why is it that we want every chapter to be good when God promises only that in the last chapter he will make all the other chapters make sense, and he doesn't promise we'll see that last chapter here?"[2]

I immediately thought back to that night when we arrived in Rockford and identified Gayle's body, and the thoughts that flashed through my mind as I stood weeping at her feet.

He continued to write, "I realized that this was either the time to lose my faith or an opportunity to show the God who gave his only Son to die for my sin that I love and trust him."

I broke down again as I discovered I had found someone else whose experience and faith paralleled my own; someone else who through sharing his own pain helped me feel a little less lonely, and gave me hope that I would one day understand why Gayle died.

What disturbed me about what he wrote was his claim that *God planned his daughter's death.* As he continued the story, he told of his feelings of despair, of trying to calm and comfort his wife, Ginny, all the while struggling to make sense of seeing his daughter dying before his very eyes. While this was happening, "Grandfather Mincaye" (the old Waodani tribesman who had taken the Saint family under his wing while they lived in Ecuador and whom his family had made an honorary family member) first asked whether

---

2. Ibid, 120.

he should protect Stephanie from the strange doctors and machines being used to treat her. Then, suddenly, Mincaye began to exclaim, "God himself is doing this." He began to see that God was taking Stephanie (affectionately known as "Star") home to be with him, and he began to reach out to other people at the hospital and urge them to seek God, too.[3]

Looking at the terrible night in hindsight, Saint wrote, "And you know what God has done through this? He changed my heart. He broke it. He shredded it. And in the process he helped me see what he sees. I thought the worst thing that could happen in life was that people would go into a Christ-less eternity. There's something worse than that. It is that our loving heavenly Father, the God and Creator of the universe, is being separated every day from those he desperately loves, and he will never be reunited with them again if what this book [the Bible] says is right."[4]

Saint was able to see the outcome of God's working in the death of his father and his four fellow missionaries decades after their murder took place. He was able to look at the man next to him, Mincaye, who had become one of the dearest people in the world to him and to his family; witness the spread of the Christian message throughout the Waodani people; be told of the tremendous boost that missionary work had received from that sacrifice forty years earlier; and realize the incredible good that had come through the violent, unjustified death of his father. Following Stephanie's death, he could see how her death had changed him for good as well.

---

3. Ibid, 119.

4. Ibid, 120.

But I could see little but the emptiness I felt inside when I thought of Gayle's death. I couldn't see any purpose in it, and while I agreed that there are worse things than death, I was not easily convinced that God *planned* Gayle's death. I only hoped that God would be able to bring good out of it as time went on. I wondered, too, if I could muster the kind of forgiveness toward the man who had murdered Gayle that Saint had toward his father's killers.

Steve Saint wrote, "We have an idea that if we do what God wants us to do, then he owes us to take the suffering away. I believed that; I don't believe that anymore."[5] Having lived as long as I had as a Christian, and having experienced many tests to my faith over the years, I think that I, too, abandoned long ago the idea that God owes his children a smooth ride. Had I not done so, I would have joined the host of people I have known over the years who, when life seemed unfair, decided that God wasn't worth trusting.

Yet, I needed to look deeper at my life and at the Scriptures if I would ever begin to see good coming from Gayle's death. At the same time, I realized that my search for understanding of God's role in Gayle's death was turning to the question of "why did he allow it" rather than "where was he?"

Remembering

The search for God's grace in Gayle's death—to understand the why in God's plan—led me to find unusual answers coming from unexpected places. One of these places was the weekly celebration of communion in our church.

---

5. Ibid, 118.

In the weeks following her death, I would listen to the person leading our thoughts in preparation for partaking in the Lord's Supper. While they spoke about Jesus on the night he was betrayed, my mind would wander to how Gayle died from a senseless act of violence, and I would ask God why he didn't save our daughter.

I could understand that God *planned* for Jesus to die. Didn't Jesus predict his suffering and his death a number of times? Sounds to me like a plan. Didn't Peter tell the crowd on the day of Pentecost, "This Jesus, delivered up according to the *definite plan and foreknowledge of God*, you crucified and killed by the hands of lawless men" (ESV, emphasis mine)? And didn't Peter go on to say that "God raised him up...and that we all are witnesses [of his resurrection]"? Jesus was *supposed* to die, so that our sins (*my* sins) could be atoned for, and then be raised to life as a sign of God's power and plan for us who believe. "But what about *Gayle*?" I thought.

The religious thing to say is that "Oh, God *did* raise her, and she is in paradise *right now* awaiting the resurrection and the judgment to come. She's in a better place. Just *believe*." And yet, in my grief I wanted her to be by my side one more time—not somewhere I couldn't see, hear or touch her.

Week after week I would sit during communion, tears flowing while I prayed and asked God, "Why didn't you make the bullets turn to the left, or to the right, and miss her? Why didn't she duck her head just in time? Why didn't she run out of the room and escape with her classmates? Jesus died an unjust death, but a death with a *purpose*, a purpose that you ordained from the beginning. *But why Gayle?*" I believed that God could have saved Gayle—but he chose not to.

Perhaps, I thought, it was so that I would have a better understanding of how God felt watching his only begotten son dying a torturous and humiliating death, seeing him suffer. Perhaps that's part of it, but I don't believe that is the end of it. Then, one day, an answer came to mind that changed me.

People who have lost a loved one can appreciate the need to remember them and the desire to see that the world doesn't forget them. Sometimes it's what gets us out of bed in the morning. And few things brought greater hope and joy to Laurel and me than someone letting us know they thought of Gayle, too. An anecdote could brighten our whole day.

What memories did I want to hold on to as dear to me?

* I wanted to hear her voice again—I could pick out her soprano in a chorus of thirty singers.
* I longed to feel her hug when I was feeling sad or discouraged.
* I remembered what made her laugh, cry and get angry. I recalled leading songs in church, and there Gayle would be in the front row—our eyes would meet, and she would stick her tongue out at me, trying to spoil my concentration.
* And I especially remembered her faith, how she lived the last days of her life—her dreams and aspirations, and the last times we were together.

Then, one Sunday, it came to me: *Does God feels this excited when we remember his Son?*

During the Lord's Supper, Jesus said, "Do this in remembrance of me." The Gospels devote more time to the last week of Jesus' life than to his birth, than to his teaching, than to any other time of his life and ministry. And his disciples remembered the last days they spent with Jesus more than any other time. As with so many other grieving people, his disciples naturally worked to remember every detail of the one who had died (and ascended to heaven), just as I struggled to remember the last time I talked to Gayle.

"Remember Jesus, raised from the dead, descended from David," Paul wrote to Timothy in 2 Timothy 2:8. I came to the conclusion, on a deeper and more intimate level than ever before, that God wants us to remember his Son and is really excited about it when we do.

I now believe that God loves and wants me to remember *Jesus* the way that *I* want people to remember *Gayle*—only more so.

God wants us to be able to pick *his Son's* voice out of the crowd of people and distractions of our lives.

God wants us to feel *his Son* embracing us when we are sad, discouraged or afraid.

God wants us to know and remember what made *Jesus* laugh, cry or get angry.

God wants us to remember that Jesus desires for us to be filled with joy and not take ourselves too seriously.

And God wants us to remember the freedom and the life we can enjoy because of what *his Son* did for us, and continues to do for us through his Holy Spirit.

I realize to this day that I may never fully comprehend why God allowed Gayle's life to end in the body at the age of twenty years, four-and-a-half months, and that we would remain in this world longer. But, as Stephen Saint shared ways that God used Stephanie's death to change him for good, I began to see how God was moving through Gayle's death—not to mention her life—in my heart for good.

Lady Gayle at Bristol Renaissance Faire (2004)

10

The Work of Love Is Never in Vain

The first book to help me to understand God's heart after Gayle's death was *The God of the Towel: Knowing the Tender Heart of God*, by Jim McGuiggan.[1] It was recommended by a friend of mine, and I began to read it sometime in May, following the tragedy. Having read the book several years before, I turned directly to the section of the book entitled "The God Who Allows Suffering" and began reading.

One of the main questions troubling me at that time was, If God *could* have spared Gayle's life and kept her here another forty years or more, then why *didn't* he? Part of the answer to this type of question McGuiggan finds in the life of John the Baptist. In Luke 7:18–23, John—the herald of the Messiah—is being held in prison by King Herod. While incarcerated, he sends some of his followers to Jesus to ask if he indeed *was* the Messiah.

While he didn't directly ask Jesus to free him from captivity, McGuiggan suggests one can almost read between the lines of John's question for Jesus. Apparently, Jesus read between those lines because he told John's followers to return and tell him what they saw (he healed people and cast out demons before their very eyes), and to pass along

---

1. Jim McGuiggan, *The God of the Towel: Knowing the Tender Heart of God* (West Monroe, LA: Howard Publishing Company, 1997).

this message: "Blessed is the one who isn't offended at me." Translation: "John, trust me."

Reading McGuiggan's meditation on the story was valuable to me, drawing my attention to how I was facing my relationship with God through the lens of my own suffering. Having already decided I could trust God after Gayle's death, though, caused me to see the story of John in prison differently. In the background to the story, John has been the forerunner of the Messiah for his entire adult life. He was baptizing and preaching in the desert, "Prepare the way for the Lord, make straight paths for him."[2] He was challenging the Pharisees and the Sadducees on their sins, and calling all men to repent. Suddenly he faces the fact that his life's work may be finished, and that his life is hanging in the balance. By sending his disciples to Jesus to ask if he is indeed the Messiah, could he really have been asking Jesus, "Was I right? Are you *really* the Messiah, or was all my labor in vain, a mistake?" Wasn't John's question just as likely a plea for affirmation as it was to be freed?

I had been told, "Joe, your work is done" when Gayle died. I was told to believe that God had taken her to be with him in paradise. I was told to accept the fact that her race was run, was finished, and that she had won the race. I had this hollow feeling in the pit of my stomach, just as John most likely did, knowing my own life, my own imperfections, and my own sins. I thought "Did Gayle really make it? Did she *really* believe in Jesus? Or, did I run my race (as a parent) in vain?" Instead of Jesus sending me witnesses to his miracles and wonders, people who knew Gayle and lived with her

---

2. Luke 3:4

were witnesses who testified to me of her life and faith (as were her journal entries). Each story encouraged me, letting me know that my work as a father was not in vain.

One of my favorite quotes from the apostle Paul is his statement to the elders of the church in Ephesus:

> "However, I consider my life worth nothing to me, if only I may finish the race and complete the task the Lord Jesus has given to me—the task of testifying to the gospel of God's grace." (Acts 20:24)

I realized that my children are the ones I most want to share the gospel of God's grace with. And the greatest reward for me isn't to see them get married and give me grandchildren—though that would be nice; it isn't to see them graduate from college magna cum laude, or even to graduate at all. The greatest reward for me has been seeing them come to their own faith in God and to desire to have an impact on others for God.

Clearly, Gayle had developed that kind of heart. In this I found great peace.

Chapter after chapter of McGuiggan's book, leading me on a survey of the Gospels and showing me God's heart with regard to suffering and loss, helped to heal the pain in my heart toward God. And more than inform me that God *cares* about our pain, sorrow and grief, his stories helped me to see my role as one who can be trusted as an agent to bring comfort and relief to others who have suffered. Perhaps that is what God had in mind for me in this all along, and perhaps serving and comforting others in their suffering could be part of the legacy that Gayle will leave in this world.

11

Moving Through Grief

You cannot stand in the same river twice. —Heracleitus

Life is like a river; events and opportunities flow past us, never to be lived or enjoyed again. It is full of so many relationships and so many choices. Sometimes we say what is on our hearts when first a feeling or thought comes to us, and sometimes we wait for a "better time." But one thing is certain: Each moment is unique, and we only live it once. In the case of Gayle and me, our moments were now over. Our chances to express our feelings to each other, where we hadn't already done so, had flowed past us forever.

The past would never return; the river future is unknown. How to continue my life without…

* the one I held in my arms and walked and sang to sleep;
* the one who actually thought I was funny;
* the one who never wanted to leave the playground when I picked her up from preschool and who protested by sucking her thumb in silence all the way home;
* the one with the sweetest and most infectious giggle in the whole world;
* the one who came home from school in fourth grade

all excited about something with the unlikely name of "Sailor Moon";[1]

* the one who accompanied me to Valentine's Day dances and didn't care that I couldn't dance in time to the music or was too tall for her;

* the one whom I taught to drive, but who would have preferred to ride horseback;

* the pretty girl who preferred wearing overalls and sweatshirts to wearing dresses;

* the one who broke bones in her ankle trying to deny an opposing player the soccer ball, even though the other girl was more than a head taller;

* the daughter I taught about God and who committed her life to God in baptism;

* the teen girl who, when other daughters were embarrassed to sit with their parents, always insisted on sitting next to me—even in public;

* the girl with the wonderful soprano voice and gift for music;

* the one who shared (most of) the same taste in music with me, and who imitated my love for books and learning;

* the one who after graduating high school went off to college and blossomed into independent womanhood more quickly than I was ready for, and of whom I was—at the same time—so proud;

* the one who went away to school for her fourth semester of college, and who seldom called me;

* and the one to whom I never got to say "good-bye"?

---

1. "Sailor Moon" is the name of a Japanese media phenomenon in which teenage girls have magical powers.

Laurel had a different list of memories—a different set of things she had and hadn't said or done with Gayle. Like me, Laurel had a lifetime of amazing and heart-warming memories, as well as a lifetime of sad ones. So many of the feelings that made up Laurel's relationship with Gayle were different from my own, and vice versa. Our mutual loss vividly illustrated to us, over the weeks and months after 2/14, the uniqueness of each relationship.

Driven by our love for each other and led by the wisdom obtained from many God-fearing people over the course of twenty-five years of marriage, we learned to listen to each other more patiently during this time. We each made the other feel safe enough to talk about how we felt by not analyzing, judging and accusing each other. Instead, we learned to appreciate and accept our differences and cherish those feelings we shared. As a result, our marriage grew stronger, and the bond we shared through the twenty years of raising Gayle held us together. Also, providing us with purpose and a common cause was our love and affection for Ryan, and our commitment to help him through the rest of his teen years and into adulthood.

Because we had so many emotional thoughts that remained undelivered to Gayle, Laurel and I suffered a great deal of grief. Neither of us had ever learned an effective way of handling loss before. Until Gayle died, I had tried a number of things over the years to help me feel better after someone died or I suffered some other kind of loss. I had tried keeping to myself. When I had been sad after losing a pet as a child, my classmates had made fun of me, and so I learned to not talk about my feelings when it came to sadness because of a loss. When I was young and my parents divorced, I thought I had to be strong for my mother—I told myself "Don't talk about how you're feeling. Can't you tell your mother is having a hard time?" (I don't remember getting this advice from anyone, but I believe I must have developed a sense of duty to hold on to the burden of sadness on my own.)

However, after Gayle's death, people in our lives seemed more interested in listening to what we had to say, and so we felt less pressure to act like we were doing better than we were. This left us free to explore and try to find out if there was any way for us to enjoy the memories we had of our daughter without the corresponding pain.

During this time, we accepted the offer of some friends from church, Stan and Jocelyn McClelland, to come and talk to us. Their son, Brandon, had been killed in a shooting several years before, and they wanted to share with us how they dealt with their loss. Stan introduced me to the book, *The Grief Recovery Handbook: The Action Program for Moving Beyond Death, Divorce, and Other Losses*, by John W. James and Russell Friedman. Stan told us about attending bereavement groups, reading various books, and the results of these and other approaches to helping him find relief after Brandon's death.

Then he shared with us about participating in a Grief❣Recovery® outreach program facilitated by someone certified by the Grief❣Recovery® Institute, which was established by the authors. This program differed from the other groups he had attended and counseling he'd received.

While other groups were made up of people who shared a similar type of loss (parents who had all lost children, in this case), the Grief❣Recovery® group included people with many different types of losses. Participating in a group with divorcees, people whose parents or siblings had died, and people who had other losses made Stan feel less isolated by his loss than he had before, and he found he had more in common with more people than he had previously thought.

Another way the program differed was in the area of its expectations. Rather than people getting together to simply talk about and remember their loved ones, the Grief❣Recovery® program taught him about specific actions he could take that would reduce the immobilizing pain he felt as a result of grief. No other group or program he had found had given him hope for this level of relief. After finishing the program, Stan was so impressed with the improvement in his overall happiness, he decided to get training to work as a Grief❣Recovery® specialist himself.

We wanted to be able to resume our lives—to begin to define what life without Gayle's physical presence would be and to continue the emotional relationship with our memories of her intact.

We obtained a copy of the *Grief Recovery Handbook* and decided to work together for our own healing from the loss of our daughter. I didn't want to wait to find a Grief❣Recovery® program in the area (Stan wasn't leading one at the time), and I had hoped our recovery would be faster than the twelve weeks that the program plans for. In the end, however—with Laurel and me working at our own pace, sharing the book and the homework exercises together—it still took roughly twelve weeks to complete the book and all the exercises. But the good news is that the program worked for us, better than anything else we had ever tried.

Following the program, we still miss Gayle. Certainly we still cry at times and feel sad at times. However, the pain associated with the things we wish we had said was gone. The regret we felt for things we hadn't done for her, or had done and later wished we could take back, no longer affected us in the same way. And the things that Gayle did that hurt us and disappointed us, and which we never got to forgive her for, no longer caused us the sadness it had before. We began to notice that the memories that had been too painful to enjoy, we were able to enjoy once more.

As a side note, many people wonder about our feelings toward the gunman and his family. This is a natural question, and I will touch on it momentarily here.

Our relationship with the gunman began the moment he entered the classroom and ended when he killed himself. The unspeakable act that he performed in killing our daughter and her classmates, and wounding many others who since have become friends of ours, left us with a great deal of intense anger.

The fact that he took his own life immediately afterward left us with a great deal of frustration as well as a sense of satisfaction in knowing he had carried out his own execution. The frustration came from knowing we would never be able to confront our daughter's murderer. This was felt in the form of grief.

This grief included anger over his robbing me of

* walking Gayle through the airport on her way to spend a year studying overseas;
* seeing her walk across the stage to receive her college diploma;
* walking her down the aisle to give her to a young man to love, protect and provide for her;
* holding her children;
* and seeing her become a mature woman and friend.

Shortly after completing our relationship to the pain caused by Gayle's death, Laurel and I used the same tools to recover from the grief associated with her killer. As the majority of the emotions we had connected with him were negative, that meant we had to forgive him in order to move on. Grief♥Recovery® taught us how to do this, and while the actions of forgiveness were difficult, we believe that living with the pain associated with our anger toward him for the remainder of our lives would have been far more difficult.

While some people might see our forgiving him as "noble" and "Christian," we also look at it as the best thing to do. Jesus taught that we are to forgive others in order to be forgiven, and in recognition of the forgiveness we have received.[2] In addition, when we hold on to anger toward someone who has hurt us without resolving it through forgiveness, no one is hurt by that anger or bitterness but ourselves.

---

2. Matthew 6:14, 18:21–35

Many confuse forgiving with forgetting or condoning. These are totally different concepts. In forgiving him for killing our daughter, we took responsibility for our response to his actions, and took actions that freed us from the power of his actions to affect our happiness and ability to live life to the full. Having enjoyed the peace that this has brought to us, we only hope that others will be able to enjoy this freedom as well.

The Dubowski family at the Grand Canyon

12

Learning to Turn Cartwheels

*Gayle would come over every Wednesday at 2 o'clock to
hang out and read the Bible together. She was always wanting to learn things from me. She would ask me to teach her
different scriptures, how to study the Bible with people.... A
few weeks ago, she asked me, "Can you teach me how to make
a difference?"*

*I gave a little laugh and said, "I think you do make a dif-
ference, Gayle."*

*"No," she replied, "because I never know the right ques-
tions to ask, and I'm too quiet, and never know what to say."*

*Looking at all of you here tonight, I think it's obvious
Gayle made a difference—and she didn't even have to try.
This is what she did when she thought she wasn't doing any-
thing.... It is really humbling...the impact of her life.*

—Stephanie Sullivan, at Gayle's memorial service

Knowing Gayle, she could never imagine how much of
an impact on other people's lives she would make and how
much she would one day be missed. Also, knowing Gayle, I
don't think she'd be altogether crazy about someone writing
a book that talks so much about her—even if that someone
is her dad. On the other hand, she's not here to stop me, so
I think I can get away with it.

Driving home from DeKalb on the morning after the
shootings, it was difficult to imagine anything positive

coming out of what we'd been through and what lay ahead. Turning things over in my mind, I thought about and mentioned to Laurel the passage in 2 Corinthians 1 where the apostle Paul writes to the church in Corinth:

> Blessed be the God and Father of our Lord Jesus Christ, the Father of mercies and God of all comfort, who comforts us in all our affliction, so that we may be able to comfort those who are in any affliction, with the comfort with which we ourselves are comforted by God. For as we share abundantly in Christ's sufferings, so through Christ we share abundantly in comfort too. If we are afflicted, it is for your comfort and salvation; and if we are comforted, it is for your comfort, which you experience when you patiently endure the same sufferings that we suffer. (verses 3–6, ESV)

She told me she was thinking about that passage, too. Both of us were trying to make sense of what we were going through. I was encouraged that Laurel and I were of like mind, thinking perhaps God had seen fit to prepare us for some work of service we could not see. In any case, the events and people who would shape our lives and help us through the dark days to come were being assembled by a loving and compassionate Father. And what the impact of the tragedy and the dark days to come would have on us was yet to be seen as well.

The event that forever changed our lives happened unexpectedly and with great suddenness, and it left us feeling traumatized. But, the healing and transformation that followed over the past two years was much slower, gentler—and at times, it seemed, imperceptible. The storm that was the shooting launched waves that washed away in a day the hopes, dreams and expectations of a lifetime. Then the tsunami-like waves eventually subsided to the tides that cast new shells on the beach in the moonlight, leaving the ebb and flow of everyday life.

Having now the benefit of a couple years' perspective, I can see some things that Gayle taught me both through living and through dying. While I cannot tell all the ways that I have been changed, there is no doubt that I *have* been changed, and in many ways for good.

The first way that comes to mind is that I understand better the importance of communicating. By communicating, I mean more than talking; by communicating I mean learning to listen. The people who have had the greatest impact on my life in the past two years are those who have loved me enough to listen. They laughed with me. They cried with me. They warned me. They encouraged me. They taught me the power of listening, not to solve all my problems, but to understand. Sometimes I received advice from these friends, but I never felt that they were listening in order to find out what advice to give; they were there to actively listen. As a result, I am trying to become a better listener.

Another aspect of communicating is expressing feelings at the right time—which is often when they occur. When Gayle died, the grief I felt was great because I never took the time to express my appreciation for so many things, and to let her know *why* I appreciated her. Much of the time we spent together I was in "parent mode," dispensing advice, giving unpaid lectures and judging her on how well she was doing. Along with that, there were many things she had done that hurt me, or made me feel unloved and unappreciated. There were still other things—many more—for which I felt I owed her an apology. Suddenly, the opportunity to tell her how I felt about her had expired.

I have heard and spoken to so many people in recent times who share the same kind of pain as I had felt, for the same fundamental reasons. Therefore, I am trying to build new habits of expression. I am trying to learn to tell people how I feel about them while they are alive, and to listen to them so they can do the same with me. That way, when we are parted, the parting will not be as painful for any of us.

Reading Gayle's journals, I see that she was conscious of this need for expression. She also recognized the cost involved. There were some things that she knew would be painful to say, but she prayed for the courage and tact to say them in the right way, and at the right time. Seeing that she died so unexpectedly reinforced in my mind the fact that we only have today, even this moment, and that to communicate should be one of the top priorities in our lives.

Another thing I have learned, and see as a major challenge in my life right now, is that we have an obligation to simplify the work of those we leave behind to clean up our "stuff." I see it as a challenge because I have yet to acquire the habits necessary to routinely carry it out in my own life.

When my uncle and my father died, within a little more than a year of each other, they left behind a great deal of clutter. There was so much "stuff" (papers, memorabilia, clothing, papers) to go through that it took a couple months to clean up, file, distribute and discard. They held on to so much that they hadn't used in years or could have disposed of long ago. I decided that I need to learn to travel lighter on my upcoming journeys around the sun, and not leave my loved ones muttering under their breath after I'm gone for making so much work for them.

Sitting across the table from a friend in a favorite restaurant, I told him, "I feel more alive now than I can remember feeling in a long time." This is a major improvement from the day of Gayle's funeral, when I really wanted her to move over so I could climb into the casket with her.

What brought about this freedom was, in part, knowing that I don't know what tomorrow holds for me any more than I knew what that Valentine's Day held for me. And knowing wouldn't have changed a thing. I'm learning not to worry over what the future holds, nor to fret over or relive yesterday's mistakes. Instead, I try to make each day as good as I can make it, thank God for his goodness and forgiveness, and trust in God's plans for my tomorrow.

In Gayle's journals, I read about her worries and concerns about the future: Where was she going to live the next year after her roommates moved? What was she going to major in, and what was she going to do after she graduated? Where was she going to work, and how was she going to ever afford to pay for her next semester of school if I [Dad] didn't find a job? Where was she going to travel, and what should she study abroad? All of these worries for a future that would never be.

Thinking back to my own life, I can't think of very many things I worried about turning out as bad as I worried they would. And when they did, I found that I experienced them twice—once in my imagination and the other time in real life—instead of simply once. My worry did not benefit me one iota. I remembered Jesus' words, which I memorized when I first read them long ago, "Therefore, do not worry about tomorrow, for tomorrow will worry about itself. Each day has enough trouble of its own" (Matthew 6:34). Somehow, seeing Gayle's life and its sudden end reinforced this lesson in a way that nothing else had.

When Gayle wasn't worrying, she was singing. She was reading. She was serving. She was dancing. She was laughing. She was making snow angels. I saw Gayle come alive when she wasn't preoccupied with tomorrow or yesterday, but simply enjoying what God had presented her in life at that moment. That's what led to her being able to turn cartwheels in a thunderstorm.

As time passes, I am discovering that Paul's words in 2 Corinthians 1 are ringing true for me. I've discovered that as I have received comfort and encouragement from God and from others, I have comfort and encouragement I want to pass along to others. This discovery wasn't revealed to me overnight but, rather, over the course of a couple years of searching and experience.

Our own suffering opened my eyes more to the suffering that is all around me. It opened my heart to the pain that others go through, brought about by the loss of loved ones, loss of health, loss of work, and loss of trust and faith. I have discovered the importance of listening without analyzing and judging. I have experienced the relief that genuine laughter can bring to a soul that is downcast. I have found peace in knowing that the sadness and brokenness one feels due to loss of any kind is normal. I have found a mission in life in helping others to learn to deal with loss—a skill that few of us have learned, and fewer still teach.

I hope to carry out this mission by encouraging people to communicate better with one another, to listen to and understand each other. One way to do this is through the written word. We live in a world that is divided by tools that were intended to connect us. A hundred years ago, people still wrote heart-felt letters to one another; today, our inboxes are filled with copied jokes and "e-cards." What is personal and heart-felt about a chain email? I encourage people to learn the art of heart-felt expression once more.

Of all the hundreds of cards we received from people after my father and Gayle died, the ones that meant the most to us were those in which people had written their own thoughts and feelings. They did not have to be lengthy, and most were not. But they came from the heart, whether eloquent or not. Therefore, I will encourage people to write to one another, whether by letter, by card, or (sigh!) by email. (Wouldn't you like to find that people are saving your emails—or cards, or letters—because they touched their heart?)

Part of this mission is helping people learn how to move through grief. Seeing the impact of Grief♥Recovery® on our lives, I sought training to work with grievers and have become certified as a Grief♥Recovery® specialist. I have found working with people following major losses to be some of the most rewarding work I have ever done, and I hope to continue doing so as long as there are people in need.

Finally, I am registering (on the very day I'm writing this) for classes at Northern Illinois University, from where I hope to receive a master's degree in marriage and family therapy one day. I long to not only help people recover from loss, but to help families connect with one another and navigate their life's journey with greater purpose and harmony. I want to help others discover *their* gifts and dreams, and find the path in life that will bring them meaning and fulfillment.

While Gayle's journey in this world has ended, mine continues. I see only the dots on the map of my past, the memories of my life to date. But as I continue to learn from Gayle's life (and death), I am coming to understand my own life's map better. I am learning to serve others and help them on their journeys, and I'm finding new meaning in life, more joy and renewed energy. If this keeps up, I might finally be able to do a cartwheel in the rain myself.

Acknowledgments

I began writing this book about six months after the events described herein began, and worked on it off and on for roughly a year and a half. I could not have started such a work, nor stayed with it, without the encouragement and support of many people along the way. While the list of people who helped put me and my family back together after 02/14/08 might fill a hundred pages, I am going to try to recognize as many of you as I can in four.

Let me begin with my wife, Laurel. I thank her for giving me time and permission to write, for reading and rereading multiple versions of the book (not an easy task, as the story is as much her own as it is mine), and her tender love and understanding along the way.

I also want to thank our son, Ryan, for believing that I could do it, and believing that it might make a difference in people's lives.

Given that I felt a burning need and passion to write the story wasn't enough; I needed to know that other people thought I could do so, and that it was important enough to make the necessary sacrifices to see it through. For this confidence, I thank my mother and my friend Wes for finally giving me the push I needed to get started.

This book would never have become a reality without the unselfish and professional help of my dear friend Curt Simmons. I thank him for many breakfasts and lunches, for being one of the best listeners I've ever had, for his wonderful poem, and for the many weeks spent editing some very lengthy drafts of this book, and for never giving up on it.

I thank nephews Christian and George, and niece Alisha, for their song, and for loving their family (and especially their cousin) so much. I also want to thank Shannon Kekhaev for her song, which still brings a tear to my eye whenever I listen to it.

I must also thank Robin and David Weidner for being there for us during our most difficult hours and sharing in our tears. Special thanks go to Robin for helping me clarify what the book is about, and so transforming it into a more readable form. Without her loving and gentle critiques, this book may never have become a reality.

I also want to thank Steve Hutson for his advice and encouragement, and going out of his way to help me through the process of writing a book proposal and finding people to consider publishing it.

After working for well over a year on the book, I reached out to friends to find out whether I had said what I meant to say. I want to thank my sister Liz, my mother, Edith, and friends Rebekah, Cindy, Barb, John, Scott, and Brenda; Russell Friedman of the Grief Recovery Institute; and Sheila Jones's friends Farrar Moore and Sheryl Cook of Caring Resources. I owe you thanks for encouraging me to finish the work, and letting me know that it was worthwhile.

Before I could begin writing, I needed to go through the experience and deal with the impact of the events that changed our lives in the first place. Just as writing the book was the result of a lot of input and emotional support, so was the recovery.

I must begin by thanking Jeff and Roberta Balsom, who loved and listened to us, and who helped us every step of the way, and who have become like brother and sister to us. Jeff was with me when the story began and is by my side to this day. Next, for sharing with us about *The Grief Recovery Handbook,* and their own story, I thank Stan and Jocelyn McClelland and for their love and friendship.

Along with them, I thank all the people who shared in the journey with us—including the physical journeys to DeKalb and Rockford one cold night: Jeff, James, Ed, Curt, Jim, Kathleen, Mark and Allison, as well as the members of the DeKalb Church of Christ. I also thank our church group back in Carol Stream for your prayers on our behalf, and the hundred or so people who came to see us when we returned home.

I thank the staff and owners of Salerno's Rosedale Chapels and Glenbard North High School (Gayle's alma mater) for hosting the funeral and memorial service, and the Chicago Church of Christ for making the memorial service as amazing as it was. The outpouring of love from my former coworkers and employers, the many of people in the community, and those who traveled from miles away to celebrate Gayle's life, and to share in our sorrow, will always amaze and inspire me.

I thank Steve Lux for becoming the friend he has been to us, and for having such a soft spot in his heart for our firstborn. I thank John and Barbara Peters for their love and support, and the NIU administration, faculty and staff for the memorials and days of remembrance they have put on since 2/14, as well as for taking the hassles out of all the arrangements and financial aspects of life after the shooting. Our family thanks the anthropology department for setting up the annual grant in Gayle's honor, and the university and the many donors for starting the Forward Together Forward Scholarship at NIU. Special thanks goes to Scott Peska, Sheryl Frye, Megan Gerken and the staff of the Office of Support and Advocacy at NIU, as well as all the student volunteers who have helped our family.

To the NIU and DeKalb Police, DeKalb Fire Department, and all the medical personnel at Kishwaukee Community Hospital, Air Angels, and St. Anthony Medical Center in Rockford, Illinois, who valiantly tried to save as many as possible, thanks. To Drew Wells—thanks for becoming our friend.

Thanks also to Rosemary Smith, author of *Children of the Dome*, as well as the minister from the Morning Star Baptist Church who sent us books and other materials, and all the other people who generously gave gifts to us in Gayle's honor. I also thank Randy Jordan and HOPE *worldwide* for setting up the fund in Gayle's name.

Finally, thanks to Sheila Jones and DPI Books for your eagerness to work on this book, and to work on it so quickly. Thanks for your insight, and for believing in the value of this story. And thanks to all those who helped her to put it all together.

Above all, thanks to God for his abundant grace, even in the wake of the unthinkable.

Part 3

Appendix

Lyrics, Poems, Remembrances

I was Gayle's UNIV 101 instructor in the fall of 2006. Gayle was a special and unique student. I remember her mostly from her engaging smile. It could be tough to know if she was smiling with you, at you, or to herself as if there was a private joke going on in her head.

A bit shy, a wry sense of humor, and a quiet confidence were things that I'll always remember about Gayle. She saw things for what they were and was unafraid to be critical. If there was an assignment that she felt was "silly" or "pointless," she didn't do it and didn't care what you thought about it.

She always sat near the front—a trait that I'm afraid was possibly a part of why she was so much in harm's way on that fateful Thursday afternoon. I only ran into Gayle a few times since that class ended in November of 2006, but I will never forget her. She had an infectious smile and a touch of impishness.

Farewell, Gayle. Please watch over your brother and parents as they try to continue their lives without you.

—Steve Lux, NIU

Well Done

A Poem by Curt Simmons

I have your daughter in my arms, she's one amazing girl
A beautiful addition here, a rare and priceless pearl.

My heart was overwhelmed with joy, when first I saw her face.
I held her hand and softly said, "Well done, you've won the race."

I drew her close and smiled at her, then hugged her very tight.
I told her I was proud of her for how she fought the fight.

I told her, "Go and look around, it's wonderful up here."
"It's your reward for serving Me, it's all for you, my dear."

She asked about the two of you, concerned that you're okay.
I promised her I'd meet your needs and help you every day.

I opened up the Book of Life and showed her both your names.
I told her that your faith was real, your life backs up your claims.

She smiled as wide as possible, and said she knew it well.
That you were both her heroes, and she then went on to tell.

Of the many glowing stories about how you set the tone
For her to one day call Me "Lord" from examples you had shown.

Of course, I wasn't caught off guard, I knew it all was true.
The two of you are known up here for all you say and do.

Then I said, "It's time for us to go and view your mansion fair.
I built it just with you in mind, with extra special care."

She leaped for joy and gratitude when first it caught her eye.
She couldn't quite believe that it was true and not a lie.

But nothing like the joy she felt when I told her, "Wait, there's
    more!"
"The mansions for your mom and dad I'm building right next
    door."

It was the first of my encounters here, with your lovely daughter
    Gayle.
She's wonderful in every way, your efforts did not fail.

And though I never thought that we could take our singing higher
It really has improved a bit since Gayle has joined the choir.

She loves it here in Paradise, she's having quite a blast
Enjoying life eternal while rejoicing in her past.

She misses you so very much and wants to let you know
That underneath your loving care her faith was bound to grow.

She loves you more than ever now, for what you gave to her.
She brags about you constantly, yes this I can confer.

I understand your present pain and why you deeply grieve.
I understand how hard it was to see you daughter leave.

But rest assured she's still alive, she crossed the finish line.
My deepest thanks to both of you for raising her so fine.

You paved the way for Gayle to live, you showed her how to run
The greatest race that's known to man, to you I say, "Well done!"

A Song for Gayle: Keep on Smiling

Song Lyrics by Shannon Kekhaev

Never knew how much you meant to me
'Til the day you were gone
Can't find words for the way I'm feeling
So I'm singing this song.

The things I know right now
At least the ones I can express
I Miss you
And your smile I'll never forget.

So keep on smilin'
Keep on singin' the way you do
And keep on lovin'
Cuz we'll keep lovin' you
We'll keep lovin' you.

Your heart so pure
Your spirit so sweet
You're a shining star
To everyone you'd meet

And the only thing that keeps me
Halfway getting through
Is knowing where you are
And that I'll be there one day, too.

So keep on smilin'
Keep on singin' the way you do
And keep on lovin'
Cuz we'll keep lovin' you
We'll keep lovin' you.

Hey, Love (Gayle's Song)

*Song written, performed and recorded
by George and Alisha Balogi, and
Christian Ramaker*[1]

It's hard to say good-bye,
we don't have time to say.
It feels like you're still here,
but as we wipe away our tears.

Hey, Love. You can hardly imagine
how much you're missed down here.
Hey, Love, take our prayers to heaven;
you'll always be a breath of fresh air.

You lived with your heart;
your smile lights us up.
Your eyes were oh so dear,
we remember them so clear.

The Spirit lifts you up.
Surrounded by peace and love,
your life is just begun—
we'll see you in Heaven.

Hey, Love. You can hardly imagine
how much you're missed down here.
Hey, Love, take our prayers to heaven;
you'll always be a breath of fresh air.

---

1. ©2008 - George Balogi, Christian Ramaker, and Alisha Balogi. Available for preview and download on www.cdbaby.com for $1. Profits from the sale of the song will be donated to the HOPE worldwide fund in honor of Gayle.

Days come and go,
still we'll never know
what God wants for us
while we're here.

You're better now,
so much better now;
even so we wipe
away our tears.

Hey, Love. You can hardly imagine
how much you're missed down here.
Hey, Love, take our prayers to heaven;
you'll always be a breath of fresh air.

Suggested Resources

Books

James, John W., and Russell Friedman. *Grief Recovery Handbook: The Action Guide for Moving Beyond Death, Divorce, and Other Losses (20th Anniversary Expanded Edition).* New York: HarperCollins Publishers, Inc., 2009.

James, John W., and Russell Friedman, with Dr. Leslie Landon Matthews. *When Children Grieve: For Adults to Help Children Deal with Death, Divorce, Pet Loss, Moving, and Other Losses.* New York: HarperCollins Publishers, Inc., 2001.

Stillwell, Elaine E. *The Death of a Child: Reflections for Grieving Parents.* Skokie, IL: ACTA Publications, 2004.

Walton, Charlie. *When There are No Words: Finding Your Way to Cope with Loss and Grief.* Ventura, CA: Pathfinder Publishing of CA, 1996.

Smith, Rosemary. *Children of the Dome: Twenty-eight True Stories of Survival and Hope after the Loss of a Child.* Oxnard, CA: Pathfinder Publishing of CA, 1999.

Piper, John, and Justin Taylor, ed. *Suffering and the Sovereignty of God.* Wheaton, IL: Crossway Books, 2006.

Sittser, Jerry. *A Grace Disguised: How the Soul Grows Through Loss (Expanded Edition).* Grand Rapids, MI: Zondervan, 2004.

McGuiggan, Jim. *The God of the Towel: Knowing the Tender Heart of God.* West Monroe, LA: Howard Publishing Company, Inc., 1997.

Van Ryn, Don and Susie, Newell Colleen and Whitney Cerak, with Mark Tabb. *Mistaken Identity: Two Families, One Survivor, Unwavering Hope.* New York: Howard Books, a division of Simon & Schuster, Inc., 2008.

Internet

www.grief-recovery.com – the Grief Recovery Institute

www.facebook.com – You can comment on the book by visiting the Gayle Dubowski Memorial page in Facebook.

Email - You can communicate by email with the author at CartwheelsintheRain.Dubowski@gmail.com.

Donations

Gifts we received after Gayle's death were donated to HOPE *worldwide* and designated for use by youth programs for children in the republics of the former Soviet Union. Each year interest accrued by the **Gayle Dubowski Fund for Youth** will be distributed as needed by HOPE *worldwide* to meet needs of orphans and under-privileged children. As the fund grows, so will the good that it will provide for these people in the future.

If anyone would like to contribute to this fund, simply send the gift to
Gayle Dubowski Fund for Youth
c/o HOPE *worldwide*
353 W. Lancaster Ave.
Suite 200
Wayne. PA 19087
Attn: Donation Processing

Be sure to include "Gayle Dubowski Fund for Youth" in the memo field of the check or money order.

In addition, the song "Hey, Love (Gayle's Song)" (©2008 Copyright-George Balogi, Christian Ramaker, and Alisha Balogi) is available for preview and MP3 download from www.cdbaby.com for $1. Profits from the sale of the song will be donated to the HOPE *worldwide* fund mentioned above.